TILLIE OLSEN was born in Nebraska in 1913 and has lived for most of her life in San Francisco. Her education was cut short by the Depression: she wrote and published when young, but the necessity of working full time while raising and supporting four children prevented her from writing for twenty years. She was in her mid-forties before she began again.

Tillie Olsen has taught at Amherst College, Stanford University, was Writer-in-Residence at the Massachusetts Institute of Technology, Distinguished Visiting Professor at the University of Massachusetts in Boston, and a Fellow of the Radcliffe Institute. She has received both Ford Foundation and National Endowment for the Arts grants, a Guggenheim Fellowship, and an award for Distinguished Contribution to American Literature from the American Academy and the National Institute of Arts and Letters. In 1979 she was awarded an honorary doctorate in Arts and Letters from the University of Nebraska, and in 1982 an honorary doctorate in Literature by Knox College. Her works of fiction include *Tell Me a Riddle* (1962), three short stories and a novella, and *Yonnondio* (1974), her 'lost' novel published forty years after its opening chapter appeared in an early *Partisan Review*. Her first work of non-fiction, *Silences*, was published in America in 1979. All are published by Virago.

She continues to write, and lives in San Francisco, California.

D0415795

Mother to Daughter

Daughter to Mother

Mothers on Mothering

A reader & diary

SELECTED AND SHAPED BY

TILLIE OLSEN

Published by VIRAGO PRESS Limited 1985
41 William IV Street, London WC2N 4DB

Copyright © 1984 The Feminist Press

First published by The Feminist Press,
Old Westbury, New York 1984

British Library Cataloguing in Publication Data

Mother to daughter, daughter to mother: a diary and reader.
1. Mothers and daughters — Literary collections
2. English literature — 20th century
I. Olsen, Tillie
820.8'0353   PR1111.M6

ISBN 0-860687-21-X

Printed in Great Britain
Anchor Brendon Ltd, Tiptree, Essex

CONTENTS

A NOTE ABOUT THIS BOOK

This small book comes out of years and years of reading on its subject so central to my life; of gathering, storing, sharing passages and work which gave to me sustenance, human beauty and anguish, understanding and self-knowledge.

It does not pretend to be more than it is—partial (in both senses of the word): resonant with presences, but perhaps most eloquent in its absences, its silences, its indications of what yet needs to be written (and in its spaces awaiting your words).

Some of the writers herein are renowned (although this aspect of their work may surprise); others are little or not at all known, or are in eclipse. To chord these latter with the instantly recognizable names, to indicate their contribution, was a motive force for this book.

Most of what has been, is, between mothers, daughters, and in motherhood, in daughterhood, has never been recorded, nor (even as yet) written with comprehension in our own voices, out of our own lives and truths. What does exist is a small, perhaps the smallest portion of all literature. Nearly all of it is recent and, not surprisingly, primarily the contribution of women in the first generation of their families to emerge into written literature—and mostly of working class origins, Scandinavian, Canadian, women of color.

Least present is work written by mothers themselves (although each year sees more). Whatever the differences now (including literacy, small families), for too many of the old, old reasons, few mothers while in the everyday welter of motherhood life, or after, are writing it. That everyday welter, the

A Note about This Book

sense of its troublous context, the voice of the mother herself, are the largest absences in this book. And elsewhere.

By its very nature, a small daybook could not have the fullness of anthology (scope, breadth, intensity, focus— yes). Much has had to be excerpts. The necessity for, the task of this excerpting (absences again) has been painful. I have tried to be responsible to the original. My primary care and concern has been that essence, integrity, individual quality, remain; my intention (and comfort) that if the work is not familiar, readers would seek out the original (named in the Sources section) and make the whole their own. And go on to other work by that writer.

This small reader, then, constitutes a very large reading list. But again partial. Other work as essential and as cherished (including some by writers in the book) is absent. They were not excerptable, or available, or there was not room. For readers, for teachers, for anthologizers, it is important that at least some of these have presence here:

The mother/daughter intertwining or the motherhood experience in *This Child's Gonna Live* by Sarah Wright, *Fables for Parents, The Homemaker,* "Babushka Farnham," and "The Forgotten Mother" by Dorothy Canfield Fisher, *Women and Appletrees* by Moa Martinson, *The Man Who Loved Children* by Christina Stead, *The Firedwellers* and story collections by Margaret Laurence, the early Margaret Drabble, Mrs. Gaskell and Jane Austen, Alice Munro, Sheila Ballantyne, Jayne Anne Phillips, Joyce Maynard, Joan Chase, Rosellen Brown, Kim Chernin, and Betty Smith. Also, *Cast a Wistful Eye* by Martha Stephens, *Natural Childbirth* by Toi Derricotte, *Garden of Eros* by Dorothy Bryant, "Still Life with Fruit" and "The Mother-in-law" by Doris Betts, *Hearts* by Hilma Wolitzer, *Housekeeping* by Marilynne Robinson, *Keeper of Accounts* by Irena Klepfisz, *Child of the Dark* by Caroline de Jesus, *Mother*

A Note about This Book

Knot by Jane Lazarre, *Between Ourselves: Letters between Mothers and Daughters* edited by Karen Payne, *Letters Home* by Sylvia Plath, letters of Madame de Sevigne to her daughter, and two classic essays by Susan Griffin in *Made from This Earth*, "Women and Children Last" and "Feminism and Motherhood".

Because certain selections in the book may not sufficiently indicate the centrality, importance, richness of the original from which they are taken (others are self-evident), I reiterate them: *Old Woman at Play* by Adele Wiseman, *The Dollmaker* by Harriette Arnow, *Of Woman Born: Motherhood as Experience and Institution* by Adrienne Rich, *Momma, A Start on All the Untold Stories* by Alta, *A Book about My Mother* by Toby Talbot, *The Joys of Motherhood* by Buchi Emecheta, the Partisan section in Bryna Bar Oni's memoir *The Vapor*, the long elegy to her mother in Sharon Doubiago's *Hard Country*, and every word of Adeline Naiman's "Jennie Lubell Is in a Nursing Home in Provincetown".

Tillie Olsen

JANUARY
Mother to Daughter: Her Own Voice

Darling, life is not in my hands . . .
I cannot promise very much . . .

I promise you love. Time will not take away that.

Anne Sexton

go quickly, Tsukiko,

                     into your circled dance
go quickly

                     before your steps are
                     halted by who you are not
go quickly

                     to who you are . . .

Janice Mirikitani

I am giving you the dark birds of the night
yes, they are mine, they are mine to give

Michele Murray

You who were darkness warmed my flesh
where out of darkness rose the seed.
Then all a world I made in me;
all the world you hear and see
hung upon my dreaming blood.

There moved the multitudinous stars,
and coloured birds and fishes moved.
There swam the sliding continents.
All time lay rolled in me, and sense,
and love that knew not its beloved.

O node and focus of the world;
I hold you deep within that well
you shall escape and not escape—
that mirrors still your sleeping shape;
that nurtures still your crescent cell.

I wither and you break from me;
yet though you dance in living light
I am the earth, I am the root,
I am the stem that fed the fruit,
the link that joins you to the night.

Judith Wright

Rebecca, sweet-one, little-one
Siobhain Levy, fur-pie, loveliness,
sweet-face, sleepy head, Becca,
Becalla, lovely-one, loved-one,
sweet-pie, my favorite, my dear
one, nudnik, silly-face, sweetness,
dear-heart, little terror, little
madness, how many messages you
draw for me,
I love you Mommy
Becky, love, love, Becky, Love
I hate you Mommy
dark eyes
dark eyes
all those secrets you
give me
(*Don't tell my teacher, they*
write it on a form, they
put it in a file for
hundreds to read.)
and I
hot repository of
all your moods
have birthed you
quick and
shocking creature
you run
like a needle
through my life.

Susan Griffin

Precepts for the guidance of a daughter

1. Remember Evelyn was *not* the first Norman King of England.
2. Wash your hands.
3. *When* you have washed them, hold a book in them.
4. Diminish your calves.
5. Pluck your arms.
6. Don't have the same thing said of you that was said of Master Philip.
7. Get up early, but not *too* early.
8. Talk German so fast that no one can ascertain whether you speak grammatically or no.
9. Don't gobble; it turns maidens and turkey-cocks purple.
10. Remember John Still.
11. Don't talk like Scott & Adsheads' about young men's dress.
12. Forget ties and studs for one *little* week.
13. Don't swear.
14. Assume the power of reading, if you have it not.
15. Hold your book right way up. N.B. you may know which is the right way by examining at what end of a page the numbers occur. Where the numbers are that is the top; to be held *away* from you.
16. Not to make a sequence.
17. Not to leave your room like a hay-field, of which the grass *is* gowns & brushes.
18. Not to take pocket-handkerchiefs for articles of virtue.

    Altogether to conduct herself as becomes the daughter of E. C. Gaskell & sister of M. E. Gaskell.

Elizabeth Gaskell, c. 1850

SENT FROM THE CAPITAL
TO HER ELDER DAUGHTER

More than the gems
Locked away and treasured
In his comb-box
By the God of the Sea,
I prize you, my daughter.
But we are of this world
And such is its way!
Summoned by your man,
Obedient, you journeyed
To the far-off land of Koshi.
Since we parted,
Like a spreading vine,
Your eyebrows, pencil-arched,
Like waves about to break,
Have flitted before my eyes,
Bobbing like tiny boats.
Such is my yearning for you
That this body, time-riddled,
May well not bear the strain.

Lady Otomo of Sakanoue,
8th Century

Mother to Daughter: Her Own Voice

for my daughter

We love with great difficulty
spinning in one place
afraid to create

        spaces

        new rhythm ...

go quickly, Tsukiko,

        into your circled dance

go quickly

        before your steps are
        halted by who you are not

go quickly

        to learn the mixed
        sounds of your tongue,

go quickly

        to who you are ...
        Janice Mirikitani

JANUARY

for jane at thirteen

Papers in order; your face
accurate and on guard in the cardboard house
and the difficult patois you will speak
half-mastered in your jaw;
the funny make-up in your funny pocketbook—
pale lipstick, half a dozen lotions
to save your cloudless skin
in that uncertain sea
where no one charts the laws—
of course you do not belong to me
nor I to you
and everything is only true in mirrors.

I help to lock your baggage:
history book, lace collar and pink pearls
from the five-and-ten,
an expurgated text
of how the gods behaved on Mount Olympus,

and pennies in your shoes.
You lean as bland as sunshine on the rails.
Whatever's next—
the old oncoming uses
of your new troughs and swells—
is coin for trading among girls
in gym suits and geometry classes.

How can you know I traveled here,
stunned, like you, by my reflection
in forest pools;
hunted among the laurel

8

and whispered to by swans
in accents of my own invention?

It is a dangerous time.
The water rocks away the timber
and here is your visa stamped in red.
You lean down your confident head.
We exchange kisses; I call your name
and wave you off as the bridge goes under.

Maxine Kumin

FOR MY DAUGHTER'S TWENTY–FIRST BIRTHDAY

I stroked her cheek with my finger
and she began to suck for dear life
like a fish in the last stages of suffocation above water.
When I poured my voice down to revive her
she grinned and graduated from college
Summa Cum Laude, schools of minnows parting before her.
"You are not a fish," I said to her.
"You are my daughter, and just born, too.
You should know your place.
At least we are going to start off right."
Like a woman whose hand has just been severed at the wrist
but who can still feel pain winking in the lost fingers,
I felt my stomach turn when she moved in her crib of
    seaweeds.
"Last month at this time," I said,
"you and my heart swam together like a pair of mackerel."
But she waved goodbye from a moving car,
hanging onto her straw hat with one hand,
light reflecting from the car window
as from an opened geode.
I wonder if she knows how I have stood for years
staring down through the fathoms between us
where her new body swims, paying out silver light. . . .

Jeanne Murray Walker

Brushing out my daughter's dark
silken hair before the mirror
I see the grey gleaming on my head,
the silver-haired servant behind her. Why is it
just as we begin to go
they begin to arrive, the fold in my neck
clarifying as the fine bones of her
hips sharpen? As my skin shows
its dry pitting, she opens like a small
pale flower on the tip of a cactus;
as my last chances to bear a child
are falling through my body, the duds among them,
her full purse of eggs, round and
firm as hard-boiled yolks, is about
to snap its clasp. I brush her tangled
fragrant hair at bedtime. It's an old
story—the oldest we have on our planet—
the story of replacement.

Sharon Olds

I long to put the experience of fifty years at once into your
young lives, to give you at once the key of that treasure chamber
every gem of which has cost me tears and struggles and prayers,
but you must work for these inward treasures yourselves.

Harriet Beecher Stowe
to her twin daughters (1861)

11

What can I say, but that it's not easy?
I cannot lift the stones out of your way,
And I can't cry your bitter tears for you.
I would if I could, what can I say?

But we're not one, we're worlds apart.
You and I,
Child of my body, bone of my bone,
Apple of my eye.

Like a young tree, I see you sway and bend,
And I'm so afraid, afraid you might break,
Tossed by the wind, the storms that come your way,
And careless strangers, seeing fruit, who reach out to
    take. . . .

But we're not one, we're worlds apart.
You and I,
Child of my body, bone of my bone,
Apple of my eye.

Rosalie Sorrels

TO CATHY

That I not be a restless ghost
Who haunts your footsteps as they pass
Beyond the point where you have left
Me standing in the newsprung grass,

You must be free to take a path
Whose end I feel no need to know,
No irking fever to be sure
You went where I would have you go. . . .

So you can go without regret
Away from this familiar land,
Leaving your kiss upon my hair
And all the future in your hands.

Margaret Mead

My hazard wouldn't be yours, not ever;
But every doom, like a hazelnut, comes down
To its own worm. So I am rocking here
Like any granny with her apron over her head
Saying, lordy me. It's my trouble.
There's nothing to be learned this way.
If I heard a girl crying help
I would go to save her;
But you hardly ever hear those words.
Dear children, you must try to say
Something when you are in need.
Don't confuse hunger with greed;
And don't wait until you are dead.

Ruth Stone

13

each time I order her to go
for a ruler and face her small
grubby outstretched palm
i feel before hitting it
the sting in my own
and become my mother
preparing to chastise me
on a gloomy Saturday afternoon
long ago, and glaring down into my own sad
and grieving face i forgive myself
for whatever crime i may
have done. as i wish i could always
forgive myself
then as now.

Alice Walker

to Laura at eleven

Your mother's often gone,
Even when she scolds you;

What she cooks sometimes
Tastes bitter as history;

She wears books on her fingers
Instead of rings. . . .

Time is set by hands I cannot push alone,
And both of us are set to ordeal trials.

Some cannot walk through fire unburned,
Some cannot swim when weighted down with lead.

14

In daytime, I consider how to breathe,
Pace myself; a too-quick burst of speed,
A glance aside,
And I shall fall. . . .

Having perceived my strange
long-distance run,

You may become
A passionate mover of Time

Or, a passionate baker
Of chocolate cakes.

Eleven years ago, I filled myself
Complete with mother's greed,
And then I gave you to yourself. . . .

This is the painful part of growing:
Compassion for the child not yet its own.

This is the painful part of growing:
Compassion for the mother
secret from you.

Kay Keeshan Hamod

Daughter-my-mother
you have observed my worst.
Holding me together at your expense
has made you burn cool. . . .

Daughter, you lived through
my difficult affairs
as I tried to console
your burnt-out childhood.
We coped with our fathers
compared notes
on the old one and the cold one,
learned to moderate our hates.
Risible in suffering
we grew up together.

Mother-my-daughter
I have been blessed
on both sides of my life.
Forgive me if sometimes
like my fading father
I see you as one. . . .

I lean on the bosom
of that double mother
the ghost by night, the girl by day,
I between my
two mild furies
alone but comforted.

And I will whisper blithely
in your dreams

when you are as old as I
my hard time over.
Meanwhile, keep warm
your love, your bed
and your wise heart and head
my good daughter.

Carolyn Kizer

I am giving you the dark birds of night—
yes, they are mine, they are mine to give!
I am giving you your dreams unscissored—
not the cloth of remembrance
to fade in the sun . . .
Not only the moon dancing but grass dancing too
back & forth, down & across, over & under,
the dance of weaving & the thread thrown free!
Slow dream dancing of darkness
& animal breath when the tall trees whip
above me & the sleepers sleep.
Bee dancing in a golden stream
through the walls of houses,
through the windows of skins,
through the closed doors of bone,
the papery hive oozing its thick honey
& the swarm swimming on its cape of air.
Ship dancing when the wind comes fourfold
& the ship perched no heavier on the salt rim
than the weight of its following terns sky-sailing
is blown outward on its wind-winged sails
into the clouds that mask the mother moon
and part to give you what you wake not to see.
This is the dark body of the night
that turns its back to your eyes
and waits
and sings
the song of jars
the song of transformations
and the harsh owl opens to the moon
the song in its throat,

18

offers a jagged piece of night in talons
if you can reach out your hand to it. . . .

Go
I am singing the snake of my own dream
rocking
and singing

Michele Murray

1

2

3

4

5

6

7

8

9

10

11

12

13

14

15

16

17

18

19

20

21

22

23

24

25

26

27

28

29

30

31

FEBRUARY
Daughter to Mother

mother, i have worn your name like a shield.
it has torn but protected me all these years ...
Lucille Clifton

"I think my life began with waking up and loving
my mother's face."
Mirah in George Eliot's "Daniel Deronda"

O my mother ...
I still hear something new
in your increasing love!
Nelly Sachs

twenty-one years of my life you have been
the lost color in my eye. my secret blindness,
all my seeings turned grey with your going.
mother, i have worn your name like a shield.
it has torn but protected me all these years,
now even your absence comes of age.
i put on a dress called woman for this day
but i am not grown away from you
whatever i say.

Lucille Clifton

You are like an everlasting friendship.
You are like a secret almost too wonderful to keep.
You are like the beginning, end, and everything in between.
You are like a spring shower.
You are like the sun shining on me and keeping me warm.
You are like a wild flower in a meadow.
You are like a very knowledgeable volume of encyclopedias.
You are like you and I love you.

Laurel O. Hoye, age 8
(This to represent all the labored over
poems, handwritten and illustrated by
small daughters for their mothers on
Mother's Day.)

My dear, what you said was one thing
but what you sang was another, sweetly
subversive and dark as blackberries
and I became the daughter of your dream.

This body is your body, ashes now
and roses, but alive in my eyes, my breasts,
my throat, my thighs. You run in me
a tang of salt in the creek waters of my blood,

you sing in my mind like wine. What you
did not dare in your life you dare in mine.

Marge Piercy

I dream red dreams, an oasis of fire and light.
Big Grandmother calls my mother on the phone
and I answer: "Ma, ah Ai Poo wah, she wants
to talk to you," and I filter away . . .

Ai Poo and Ma are talking now to each other.
They sing and gossip and share pigs' tail soup, but wait!
Ai Poo has given up meat. Ma never has.
Ma loved to cook and gather us together
continuing what Bah Bah did, continuing
the tradition of feasting on poor man's food,
ricecrusts crackling in hot, boiled water. . . .

Oh, Ma. Oh, Ai Poo.
Are you listening to this daughter's tongue?
Are you singing as you have sung, earthmiles away?
And what is filial piety to mothers and grandmothers,
the greatgrandmothers I've never known?
Unbandage these eyes, unbind these feet.
Tell me: what threads memory, dream, myth, reality?

Nellie Wong

I must be very young; my mother is still singing, all the time. I am the third of four living children, but at this moment we are alone. I play beside her on the couch while she dusts the sunroom windowsills. There are five round-arched windows. The woodwork is tawny, red gold. When my mother sings the neighbour comes out of his house and into our yard and stretches himself out on the lawn. I gaze at her fine, pink face, glowing in the window light. Her dark hair has small, tight tight tight waves. They glow in the light. Everything glows. I am aglow with the rapture of the revelation that she is the most beautiful in the whole world, my mother. I am too young to ask, "Why me? How come I am chosen?" I belong to what is given. It is an intensely aesthetic pleasure, experienced, thank goodness, before the pinched and crabbed world with its penny-ruler measurements interposed its decrees that her nose is too long, her eyes too deeply set, baffling the child's intuitive perceptions, my unerring love. Thank you, formal education, thank you, herd standards, but no thank you, too. Long is the unlearning of your learning, glad the return to vision.

Adele Wiseman

MY MOTHER PIECED QUILTS

they were just meant as covers
in winter ...

        ... every morning I awoke to these
october ripened canvases
passed my hand across their cloth faces
and began to wonder how you pieced
all these together
these strips of gentle communion cotton and flannel
   nightgowns
wedding organdies
dime store velvets

how you shaped patterns square and oblong and round
positioned
balanced ...

how the thread darted in and out
galloping along the frayed edges, tucking them in
as you did us at night ...

in the evening you sat at your canvas
—our cracked linoleum floor the drawing board
me lounging on your arm
and you staking out the plan:
whether to put the lilac purple of easter against the red
   plaid of winter-going
into-spring
whether to mix a yellow with blue and white and paint
   the
corpus christi noon when my father held your hand

whether to shape a five-point star from the
somber black silk you wore to grandmother's funeral ...

oh mother you plunged me sobbing and laughing
into our past
into the river crossing at five
into the spinach fields
into the plainview cotton rows
into tuberculosis wards
into braids and muslin dresses
sewn hard and taut to withstand the thrashings of
   twenty-five years

stretched out they lay
armed/ready/shouting/celebrating

knotted with love
the quilts sing on

                      Teresa Palma Acosta

THINKING OF MY MOTHER WHO FIFTEEN YEARS LATER, HAS GONE EAST TO SEE THE LEAVES

How could my mother have known
that late October afternoon
when she found me at sixteen
crying in my mirror,

how could she have known
that her hands, lighting
on my shoulders from behind me
in the mirror, would
stay the winter,

would always be turning me
toward the tree in our backyard,
the blood-red oak we'd planted
just the year before
whose leaves were all that held,

as her hands that moment held
my arms, the last sharp
backward glances of the sun.

Judith Sornberger

A room to go to—
not lapidary windows,
but jars which hold the light of fruit,
the taste of summer, and my mother's labor.
In winter, I open the knotty pine door,
hide from sister and brothers,
read *Little Women* and *The Secret Garden*.

My mother stands at the sink all summer
as the fruits succeed each other—
strawberries, cherries, peaches, apricots, apples.
The huge blue enamelled cauldron
steams on the stove.
She wipes the sweat from her forehead
with a dishcloth.

At the center of all this ripeness,
her hands of fruit and sun.
Spearmint strained through cheesecloth.
Scalded mason jars lined up on the embroidered tablecloth.
Stacks of shiny metal lids and sealing rings
(used for gypsy bracelets at Halloween).
I sneak sweet froth skimmed from the top of jams.

Her hands stained and nicked
from all the peeling, cutting, blanching—
beautiful how she touched things,
how quickly she could thread a needle.
I'm not supposed to love her for this—
smoothing our hair, sewing our clothes,
or on her knees waxing the floor.

I see the blur of her smile,
her smile that hid so much.

33

FEBRUARY

I saw her cry only a few times,
when she could not hold us after her operations,
and when she told me once she was afraid,
and I could not look at her
for fear of her fear.

I remember the sound of the jars sealing at night
as if something were alive in each,
kicking to get out: first one jar, then another,
then a chorus of pops and smacks like frogs on a pond.
Then the careful carrying down to cellar,
and the winter choosing of fruit for breakfast.
When I chose, I chose by color not by taste.

I open the door so slowly,
feel the knots in the wood.
She told me here one day that I should cultivate desire.
I was surprised.
I had never connected my mother with desire,
and could not ask her if she meant a strong will,
or an earthly passion, or a clear heart.

I come to this room
where there is no longer fruit on the shelves . . .
A flickering leaf-veined pattern
falls on the floor
like a hand in front of a candle flame,
her hand on my forehead,
as if the last rooms of memory
hold only light.

Sue Standing

November 8. FM please and as few ads as possible. One beside my place in the kitchen where I sit in a doze in the winter sun, letting the warmth and music ooze through me. One at my bed too. I call them both *Mother's Radio.* As she lay dying her radio played, it played her to sleep, it played for my vigil, and then one day the nurse said, "Here, take it." Mother was in her coma, never, never to say again, "This is the baby," referring to me at any age. Coma that kept her under water, her gills pumping, her brain numb. I took the radio, my vigil keeper, and played it for my waking, sleeping ever since. In memoriam. It goes everywhere with me, like a dog on a leash. Took it to a love affair, peopling the bare rented room. We drank wine and ate cheese and let it play. No ads please. FM only. When I go to a mental hospital I have it in my hand. I sign myself in (voluntary commitment papers), accompanied by cigarettes and mother's radio. The hospital is suspicious of these things because they do not understand that I bring my mother with me, her cigarettes, her radio. ... I have found a station that plays the hit tunes of the 1940s, and I dance in the kitchen, snapping my fingers. ... I will die with the radio playing—last sounds. My children will hold up my books and I will say goodbye to them. I wish I hadn't taken it when she was in a coma. Maybe she regained consciousness for a moment and looked for that familiar black box. Maybe the nurse left the room for a moment and there was my mamma looking for her familiars. Maybe she could hear the nurse tell me to take it. I didn't know what I was doing. I'd never seen anyone die before. I wish I hadn't. Oh, Mama, forgive. I keep it going; it never stops. They will say of me, "Describe her, please." And you will answer, "She played the radio a lot." When I go out it plays—to keep the puppy company. It is fetal. It is her heartbeat—oh, my black sound box, I love you! Mama, mama, play on!

Anne Sexton

Backward, turn backward, O Time, in your flight,
Make me a child again, just for to-night!
Mother, come back from the echoless shore,
Take me again to your heart, as of yore;
Kiss from my forehead the furrows of care,
Smooth the few silver threads out of my hair,
Over my slumbers your loving watch keep,—
Rock me to sleep, mother, rock me to sleep.

Backward, flow backward, O tide of the years!
I am so weary of toil and of tears,—
Toil without recompense, tears all in vain,
Take them and give me my childhood again;
I have grown weary of dust and decay,
Weary of flinging my soul-wealth away,
Weary of sowing for others to reap,—
Rock me to sleep, mother, rock me to sleep.

Tired of the hollow, the base, the untrue,
Mother, O mother, my heart calls for you;
Many a summer the grass has grown green,
Blossomed and faded, our faces between,
Yet, with strong yearning and passionate pain,
Long I to-night for your presence again.
Come from the silence so long and so deep,—
Rock me to sleep, mother, rock me to sleep.

Elizabeth Akers Allen, 1860
Sung, recited, over and over
the last decades of the last century

My young mother, her face narrow
and dark with unresolved wishes
under a hatbrim of the twenties,
stood by my middleaged bed.

Still as a child pretending sleep
to a grownup watchful or calling,
I lay in a corner of my dream
staring at the mole above her lip.

Familiar mole! but that girlish look
as if I had nothing to give her—
Eyes blue—brim dark—
calling me from sleep after decades.

Jane Cooper

In sleep the other night I met you, seventeen
your first nasty marriage just annulled,
thin from your abortion, clutching a book

against your cheek and trying to look
older, trying to look middle class,
trying for a job at Wanamaker's

dressing for parties in cast off
stage costumes of your sisters. Your eyes
were hazy with dreams. You did not

notice me waving as you wandered
past and I saw your slip was showing.
You stood still while I fixed your clothes,

as if I were your mother. Remember me
combing your springy black hair, ringlets
that seemed metallic, glittering;

remember me dressing you, my seventy year
old mother who was my last dollbaby,
giving you too late what your youth had wanted.

Marge Piercy

I look at my hands, Momma
And I see yours
And those of your mother before you.
Ridged and gnarled hands
Peasant hands: fine tooled and lined
Veins running through
The blue ridge mountains

in our hands
In our breasts
Round rolling hills
Blue veined breasts
Blue rivers caressing the earth
   of my breasts
      our breasts
Legs,
Our famous Davis legs: long and thin,
Broad shoulders: swimmer's body.
No waist: a breast to hip straightaway.
My body is yours, Momma.
I am a carbon copy.
Only bigger. . . .
Dwarfing you by my size.
By the size of my body
   the body you gave me
   the body you birthed
You must sit small in its shadow
Waning.
Your body aging.
Mine growing strong.
My hands, blue-ridged, reaching up.
Your hands, white-ridged, holding on.

Laura Davis

Written during the Nazi occupation:

TO MY MOTHER

From where have you learned to wipe the
tears,
To quietly bear the pain,
To hide in your heart the cry, the hurt,
The suffering and the complaint?

Hear the wind!
Its open maw
Roars though hill and dale.
See the ocean ...
The giant rocks,
In anger and wrath it flails.

Nature all arush, agush
Breaks out of each form and fence.
From where is this quiet in your heart,
From where have you learned strength?

Hannah Senesh

O my mother,
we who dwell on an orphan star—
sighing to the end the sighs of those
who were thrust into death—
how often the sand gives way beneath your steps
and leaves you alone—

Lying in my arms
you taste the mystery
Elijah knew—
where silence speaks
birth and death occur
and the elements are mixed differently—

My arms hold you
as a wooden cart holds those ascending to heaven—
weeping wood, broken out
from its many transformations—

O you who return,
the mystery overgrown with forgetting—
I still hear something new
in your increasing love!

Nelly Sachs

1

2

3

4

5

6

7

8

9

10

11

12

13

14

15

16

17

18

19

20

21

22

23

24

25

26

27

28

MARCH
Anger, Chasms,
Estrangements

Out of her womb of pain my mother spat me.
Audre Lorde

and if only
i could walk
through this veil of fears
if my eyes weren't
cataracts
from your unshed tears
Stephanie Markman

Here,   my child with fever sleeps,
her breath light   hesitant

as a butterfly   poised between one
and another flower and   the sky:

I wait: the cord   of her breath as it
falters tightening at my   throat; her hands

are blazing, dry: I   freeze: the silenced
child I once was calls, calls for   help, but

in another city my mother   stirs, crying out

blame behind a black   door, a blank wall.
                                   Patricia Cumming

Out of her womb of pain my mother spat me
into her ill-fitting harness of despair
into her deceits
where anger re-conceived me
piercing my eyes like arrows
pointed by her nightmare
of who I was not
becoming.

Going away
she left in her place
iron maidens to protect me
and for my food
the wrinkled milk of legend
where I wandered through the lonely rooms of afternoon
wrapped in nightmares
from the Orange and Red and Yellow
Purple and Blue and Green
Fairy Books
where white witches ruled
over the empty kitchen table
and never wept
or offered gold
nor any kind enchantment
for the vanished mother
of a Black girl.   *Audre Lorde*

You taught me fear, Momma.
When I was fifteen
And it was just the two of us,
We'd cook dinner, you and I

Skirt steaks marinated in soy and garlic.
Zucchini and mushrooms and onions.
Never bread. (It was too fattening)
I poured out stories.
You poured out booze,
   Scotch rocks.
   Scotch rocks.
   Scotch rocks.
   Three times over.
Later
   I watched you drink wine with dinner
I'd sit chewing
      chewing
      chewing
Swallowing the thought
   again and again.
"Oh, she's not a _____ ."
"She can't be a _____ ."
I couldn't even think the word, Momma.
I couldn't name it.
But the fear gnawed at me . . .
Choking on my food
        my tears
        my words.
I will name it, Momma.
I will name it.
   Alcoholic.
   Alcoholic.
   Alcoholic.   *Laura Davis*

BUT WHAT I'M TRYING
TO SAY MOTHER IS

You are barely able to walk,
sewn up between your legs, bleeding,
and slumped over from the weight
of six months of pregnancy,
although it *is* all over.
You wear your green chenille robe
and carry a picture of the dead child, the fifth one.
Mother, why don't you stop looking at me?
Let me wash you, please.
And yes, I go to the cemetery.
I cry, I pray for his soul,
I pour milk on his grave,
and I do it because I loved you once, I did
and it was good.

Ai

I went around the house to the back door, thinking, I have been to a dance and a boy has walked me home and kissed me. It was all true. My life was possible. I went past the kitchen window and I saw my mother. She was sitting with her feet on the open oven door, drinking tea out of a cup without a saucer. She was just sitting and waiting for me to come home and tell her everything that had happened. And I would not do it, I never would. But when I saw the waiting kitchen, and my mother in her faded, fuzzy Paisley kimono, with her sleepy but doggedly expectant face, I understood what a mysterious and oppressive obligation I had, to be happy, and how I had almost failed it, and would be likely to fail it, every time, and she would not know. *Alice Munro*

"I'm sorry for Fern," my mother said. "I'm sorry for her life."

Her sad confidential tone warned me off.

"Maybe she'll find a new boy friend tonight."

"What do you mean? She's not after a new boy friend. She'd had enough of all that. She's going to sing 'Where'er You Walk.' She's got a lovely voice, still."

"She's getting fat."

My mother spoke to me in her grave, hopeful, lecturing voice.

"There is a change coming I think in the lives of girls and women. Yes. But it is up to us to make it come. All women have had up till now has been their connection with men. All we have had. No more lives of our own, really, than domestic animals. *He shall hold thee, when his passion shall have spent its novel force, a little closer than his dog, a little dearer than his horse.* Tennyson wrote that. It's true. *Was* true. You will want to have children, though."

That was how much she knew me.

"But I hope you will—use your brains. Use your brains. Don't be distracted. Once you make that mistake, of being— distracted, over a man, your life will never be your own. You will get the burden, a woman always does."

"There is birth control nowadays," I reminded her, and she looked at me startled, though it was she herself who had publicly embarrassed our family, writing to the Jubilee *Herald– Advance* that "prophylactic devices should be distributed to all women on public relief in Wawanash County, to help them prevent any further increase in their families." Boys at school had yelled at me, "Hey, when is your momma giving out the proplastic devices?"

"That is not enough, though of course it is a great boon and religion is the enemy of it as it is of everything that might ease the pangs of life on earth. It is self-respect I am really speaking of. Self-respect."

I did not quite get the point of this, or if I did get the point I was set up to resist it. I would have had to resist anything she told me with such earnestness, such stubborn hopefulness. Her concern about my life, which I needed and took for granted, I could not bear to have expressed. Also I felt that it was not so different from all the other advice handed out to women, to girls, advice that assumed being female made you damageable, that a certain amount of carefulness and solemn fuss and self-protection were called for, whereas men were supposed to be able to go out and take on all kinds of experiences and shuck off what they didn't want and come back proud. Without even thinking about it, I had decided to do the same.   *Alice Munro*

"Heard from Pique?"

"No." Turning away so that the old man would not see her request for reassurance.

"I thought not. You have got to quit fretting over that girl. As I keep saying.". . .

"Don't mistake me, Royland. I don't want her living here any more. She can't. She mustn't. She's got to be on her own. Anything else is no good for her and no good for me. It's just that I'd like to hear from time to time that she's okay, is all."

"You think she isn't?"

"Remember that time a year ago, when she left school and took off? . . . She was in a mental hospital in Toronto for a month. A bad trip, as they somewhat euphemistically say. She hasn't had a very easy life, Royland. I clobbered her with a hell of a situation to live in, although I never meant to. Okay, maybe everything else clobbered her, too, and I'm not God and I'm not responsible for everything. But I chose to have her, in the first place, and maybe I should've seen it would be too difficult for her. You don't think of that, at the time, or I didn't, anyway."

Pique, her long black hair spread over the hospital pillow, her face turned away from Morag, her voice low and fierce. *Can't you see I despise you? Can't you see I want you to go away? You aren't my mother. I haven't got a mother.* The nurse, candy-voiced, telling Morag it would best for her to leave and in a week or so we would see. Morag, walking on streets, not knowing where, stumbling into people, seeing only small hard-bright replayed movies inside. Pique at five saying *Tell me the story about the robin in our own dogwood tree please Mum.* Pique on the first plane flight saying *Is it safe Mum?* and Morag saying *Yes,* hoping this was true. Pique in England saying *We're going home?* and not knowing where that place could be. Pique saying *Are we really going to live on a farm and can I have a dog?* Pique, when her father visited both those times, ten years apart, and then when he had to go away again, Pique saying nothing. Nothing. Pique's face turned away, her hair spread across the white freeze-drift of hospital linen, saying *I despise you.*   *Margaret Laurence*

"Do you simply loathe us, Mother?"

And just imagine, Katinka Stordal answered, "Yes, I loathe you. You whip me through life like an animal."

"We do?"

"You do."

"So now we know," said Borghild bitterly.

"So now you know."

"We thought we were your children."

"I thought so too. One thinks so much. I had hopes and wishes for you both, I wanted all sorts of things for you. And then you turn out to be nothing more than strangers, demanding and expecting one thing after another—'We'll squeeze it out of her. That's what she's for.' And afterwards you remember only the time when I couldn't manage it, when you couldn't squeeze any more out of me. You're like all the others— pulling and pushing, pulling and pushing."

"I want to see the world, but I want to be prepared as well. You still have duties towards us, Mother. You put us into the world, it's your responsibility. And Jørgen—"

"Jorgen, yes. I wanted both of you to get away, Borghild. Well prepared, too, as far as possible. It's just that I wasn't equal to it. You get so tired of not being equal to it. You seem to get blinded by exhaustion."

. . . "What a mess you've got yourself into, Mother."

"*I've* got myself into? *I* have? Do you think I've made myself so lonely, so shut off from everything, of my own accord? Shut off from being with you? From being human? Have *I* got myself into it?"

Borghild suddenly exploded. "Imagine growing up like you! I'm not going to be like any of you. I'm going to be different."

But Katinka was maundering on again about her children, just as if Borghild were not there at all. "Their faces are so

56

childish sometimes," she said to nobody in particular, "so bewildered by life. I mustn't forget that. I must remember that their faces can suddenly become quite bewildered.

"They can say hard things. . . . They can kick you aside like an old shoe. But as soon as they really need you, you long to be of use to them. I suppose that's what it means to be a mother."

"Sit down, Mother," said Borghild, "sit down for a while."

Cora Sandel

The promises of mother—
smiles, soft fingers
children could not touch.
You and your sisters
gliding like fish
(the tank was full
of your stare) to market
to market, sun
in your scarves, the ripple
of exquisite goiters.

You never wore a hat
except in mirrors,
your eyes were violet
under the veil,
under the knotted squares
calling me child.

But I went after you,
mother to mother,
put you together
when your bones rode you
apart. Something
was always breaking
down inside you.

Save me, you sob
in a dream, but nobody
runs like a friend
to your door. And I'm
in my own garden this time,
digging a ditch
for my heart.

What
did you give me, mother,
that you want it back?
An empty book to put
my poems in, peeled
apples, Patsy dolls.

Each day I sucked
at your virtuous breasts
and I'm punished
anyhow.

Shirley Kaufman

What kind of lover have you made me, mother
who drew me into bed with you at six/at sixteen
oh, even at sixty-six you do still
lifting up the blanket with one arm
lining out the space for my body with the other

> as if our bodies still beat
> inside the same skin
> as if you never noticed
> when they cut me
> out
> from you.

What kind of lover have you made me, mother
who took belts to wipe this memory from me

> the memory of your passion
> dark & starving, spilling
> out of rooms, driving
> into my skin, cracking
> & cussing in spanish

> the think dark *f* sounds
> hard *c's* splitting
> the air like blows

> *you* would *get a rise out of me*
> *you knew it in our blood*
> *the vision   of my rebellion . . .*

What kind of lover have you made me, mother
so in love

with what is left

unrequited.   *Cherríe Moraga*

60

and
mother why did you tell me
tell me
tell me why did you lie
mother why did you teach me
teach me
to watch through a veil of fears
and where is the garden mother
I can't see the garden any more
I can feel the grass
oh I can feel the grass
but I can't see the air
no I can't see the air
I can't see the
oh I can't see no I can't
not through this veil of . . .

and long time ago now mother
you were my garden
I watched with you your sky
we saw
eye to eye
and do you blame me
blame me
if I've trampled in my panic
all your nicely tended ways
is it my fault
my fault mother
that your grass has turned to straw

and yes I remember
that a rose by any other
mother

61

and yes you told me
that the grass is always
greener
and is it my fault
my fault
that I've pushed beyond your
    railings
do you blame me
blame me mother
if a weed is just a flower
growing in the wrong garden

and if only
I could walk
through this veil of fears
if my eyes weren't
cataracts
from your unshed tears . . .
                    Stephanie Markman

One day she said to me, "Parents do not understand their
children; but it works both ways. . . ." We talked about these
misunderstandings, but in a general way. And we never returned
to the question. I would knock. I would hear a little moaning
noise, the scuffling of her slippers on the floor, another sigh,
and I would promise myself that this time I should find things
to talk about, a common ground of understanding. By the end
of five minutes the game was lost: we had so few shared
interests! I leafed through her books: we did not read the
same ones. I made her talk; I listened to her; I commented.
But since she was my mother, her unpleasant phrases irked
me more than if they had come from any other mouth. And I

62

was as rigid as I had been at twenty when she tried (with her usual clumsiness) to move on to an intimate plane. "I know you don't think me intelligent; but still, you get your vitality from me. The idea makes me happy." I should have been delighted to agree that my vitality came from her; but the beginning of her remark utterly chilled me. So we each paralysed the other.

Simone de Beauvoir

Now one by one the children came, those that were able. Too late to ask: and what did you learn with your living, Mother, and what do we need to know?

Clara, the eldest, clenched:

Pay me back, Mother, pay me back for all you took from me. Those others you crowded into your heart. The hands I needed to be for you, the heaviness, the responsibility.

Is this she? Noises the dying make, the crablike hands crawling over the covers. The ethereal singing.

She hears that music, that singing from childhood; forgotten sound—not heard since, since. . . . And the hardness breaks like a cry: Where did we lose each other, first mother, singing mother?

Annulled: the quarrels, the gibing, the harshness between; the fall into silence and the withdrawal.

I do not know you, Mother. Mother, I never knew you.

Tillie Olsen

1

2

3

4

5

6

7

8

9

10

11

12

13

14

15

16

17

18

19

20

21

22

23

24

25

26

27

28

29

30

31

APRIL

Healings, Understandings, Intimacies, Shelters

But I have peeled away your anger
down to the core of love
and look, mother
I Am
a dark temple where your true spirit rises
Audre Lorde

Ma ...
My heart, once bent and cracked, once
ashamed of your China ways.
Ma, hear me now, tell me your story
again and again.

Nellie Wong

how often
have we built each other
as shelters
against the cold
Audre Lorde

I suspect the word "central" gets closest to the general feeling I had of living so completely in her atmosphere that one never got far enough away from her to see her as a person. ... She was the whole thing; Talland House was full of her; Hyde Park Gate was full of her. ... She was keeping what I call in my shorthand the panoply of life—that which we all lived in common—in being. I see now that she was living on such an extended surface that she had not time, nor strength, to concentrate, except for a moment if one were ill or in some child's crisis, upon me, or upon anyone. ... The understanding that I now have of her position must have its say; and it shows me that a woman of forty with seven children, some of them needing grown-up attention, and four still in the nursery; and an eighth, Laura, an idiot, yet living with us; and a husband fifteen years her elder, difficult, exacting, dependent on her; I see now that a woman who had to keep all this in being and under control must have been a general presence rather than a particular person to a child of seven or eight. Can I remember ever being alone with her for more than a few minutes? Someone was always interrupting. When I think of her spontaneously she is always in a room full of people.

Virginia Woolf

My depression ... burst and release[d] a shower of other paradoxes that supported my mother in her balancing act through life. In the core of anguish, ice. Out of ice, art— starting up again like perpetually blooming roses from an old, winter grave. The private, interior world my mother hid was at the same time just what, in her pictures, she set forth for display. The reason why she kept on developing was that she could accommodate herself to refusal to grow; but how, remains a mystery.

Say not of Beauty she is good. ... I also understood, suddenly, about all those intransigent colds that my mother coddled, even after she was strong and healthy, as though it had been some delicate little girl she tended; those early bedtimes from which neither love nor duty could budge her. There'd been no real call to let myself be wounded by them. ... Coldness was not a moral question in my mother, neither good nor bad. It was more the basis for survival.   *Nancy Hale*

It was a dark winter afternoon and we were sitting with the mat frame stretched right across the two tables. [My mother] on one side and I on the other, both progging away. My back was towards the fire. She always let me sit at this side because I felt the cold so. The firelight was playing on her bent head, and as I looked at her I thought, our Kate's bonny. And at this point she looked up at me and smiled, and as she did so my thought developed and said, She's more than bonny, she's beautiful is our Kate. She bent her head again and began to hum, then shortly she was singing. She sang quietly and without strain, her favourite Thora.

> I stand in a land of roses,
> But I dream of a land of snow,
> Where you and I were happy
> In the years of long ago.
> Nightingales in the branches,
> Stars in the magic skies,
> But I only hear you singing,
> I only see your eyes.
>
> Come! come! come to me, Thora,
> Come once again and be
> Child of my dream, light of my life,
> Angel of love to me!
>
> I stand again in the North land,
> But in silence and in shame;
> Your grave is my only landmark,
> And men have forgotten my name.
> 'Tis a tale that is truer and older
> Than any the sagas tell,
> I loved you in life too little,
> I love you in death too well!

73

Speak! speak! speak to me, Thora
Speak from your Heaven to me;
Child of my dreams, love of my life,
Hope of my world to be!

Child of my dreams, love of my life. Hope of my world to
be ... Her face, the firelight, and her singing was too much. I
choked and began to cry. She stopped in surprise, and putting
her hand across the mat and stroking my head said, "Aw! lass,
don't, don't. Come on. What is it? Don't." Then she added in
a conspiratorial way, "Let's have a cup of tea and a bit of cake
afore they come in, eh?"

On that day in the kitchen with the help of the firelight and
her voice we became close, we became one. At rare moments
in our lives we touched like this. One other such moment was
two days before she died when she held me in her arms and
said, "Lass, I've been a wicked woman," and my tears washing
away every hurt she had dealt me and the love that I had tried
to bring back and supplement for the hate that I had borne
her, gave me the power to say, "You have never done a bad
thing in your life." And when I came to think about it she
really hadn't. It was my nature that revolted against her
weakness. It was my nervous, sensitive, temperament that
couldn't stand up against the rough background into which
she bore me. Yet ... she gave me some part of herself, without
which I would never have survived. She passed on to me her
sense of humour and, I like to think, a little of her humanity
and kindness of heart, these last two virtues which were large
in herself and of which she received sparingly from others.

Catherine Cookson

"Everybody used to call me Deighton's Selina but they were wrong. Because you see I'm truly your child. Remember how you used to talk about how you left home and came here alone as a girl of eighteen and was your own woman? I used to love hearing that. And that's what I want. I want it!"

Silla's pained eyes searched her adamant face, and after a long time a wistfulness softened her mouth. It was as if she'd somehow glimpsed in Selina the girl she had once been. For that moment, as the softness pervaded her and her hands lay open like a girl's on her lap, she became the girl who had stood, alone and innocent, at the ship's rail, watching the city rise glittering with promise from the sea.

"G'long," she said finally with a brusque motion. "G'long! You was always too much woman for me anyway, soul. And my own mother did say two head-bulls can't reign in a flock. G'long!" Her hand sketched a sign that was both a dismissal and a benediction.   *Paule Marshall*

APRIL

I cannot recall you gentle
yet through your heavy love
I have become
an image of your once delicate flesh
split with deceitful longings.

When strangers come and compliment me
your aged spirit takes a bow
jingling with pride
but once you hid that secret
in the center of furies
hanging me
with deep breasts and wiry hair
with your own split flesh
and long suffering eyes
buried in myths of little worth.

But I have peeled away your anger
down to the core of love
and look mother
I Am
a dark temple where your true spirit rises
beautiful
and tough as chestnut
stanchion against your nightmare of weakness
and if my eyes conceal
a squadron of conflicting rebellions
I learned from you
to define myself
through your denials.

Audre Lorde

My mother talked of breakfast or laundry
in language suited to the time and place,
rationing depths & heights so they would
last for a long life.   She planned gray hairs
& grandchildren.   Engraved with age, she
waited mine with me, and *how* I asked
was it with you so long ago?   She stirred
the jam, she did not know how to sit still,
she said it of herself, always pushing
away at what would overwhelm her, chaos,
dirt, and the unfulfilled.   "His roots
tore into the earth of my flesh," she said,
"he sprouted, splitting my shell, I cracked
with the giving of him.   And then I was nothing,
the kettle on the fire; from this
he dipped the food of life."
When had she ever before been given
such language of the untapped mines of self?
You too she said, clattering with the spoon.
I shook my head.   The heavy belly dragged me down . . .

                                        Michele Murray

APRIL

I wonder why I can't remember
Your loving hands bathing me, diapering me.
You must have given hours in my care
Yet I have the vaguest memories of moments—
The sense of your special smell,
Your green wool dress at Christmas,
The warmth of your arms and breath
As you washed my hair in the kitchen sink
Years of attention; only moments of remembrance. . . .

Perhaps I was closest to you when
I struggled to break Jess free of my womb.
Two thousand miles away, you'd have understood
The pain, the betrayal, the wanting to die—
While creating a loving wrenching bond
To this precious creature, my daughter.

You never wanted children, you often said
"Well, maybe just two . . ." and I was your seventh.
But that was okay; you didn't fool me for long.
It was part of the love/hate, the excruciating joy
Of having children which permanently altered your life.
In pain and too heavy responsibility
You raised us all to independence,
And, eventually, our own parenthood.

I want to be your daughter now,
Though I never wanted a daughter myself.
"It would be too hard to help her to womanhood."
So I thought.
But you did it.
And your love shows—
Even if the hours of it are blurred.

Katie McBain

Sitting in the dusk, weeping,
the mother becomes the child
and the child, finding her curled
in the chair, feels her tears
freeze before they form,
knowing if she cries, too,
they both must drown.

She climbs into her mother's lap
to make her play a game.
Scissors, paper, stone:
what is sharp, what tears,
what hurts like falling down?

Against her mother's beating heart
she hears, *I am stabbed*
I am torn, I am stone.
"Sing me a song." she says
patting her mother's face.
"Sing Molly Malone."

In the hollow of her mother's arms
there is nothing to cling to.
She makes a life-preserver
of an embrace and throws herself
around her mother's neck.

Celia Gilbert

There were days when my mother did washing at home. She started with the dawn and the kitchen was filled with steam and soapsuds. In the afternoon her face was thin and drawn and she complained of pains in her back. I wrung and hung out clothes or carried water from the hydrant outside. She and I were now friends and comrades, planning to buy a washing machine as we worked. We charged thirty cents a dozen pieces for washing and ironing, but the women always gave us their biggest pieces—sheets, tablecloths, overalls, shirts, and generally they threw in the thirteenth piece just for good measure. Thirteen is unlucky, but for washerwomen it is supposed to be lucky—at least they thought so.

"Marie . . . if he hits me, I'll drop dead!"

. . . I was suddenly by my mother's side, facing my father, keeping her behind me.

"Do that if you dare, you! If you dare!"

I felt my mother's frail body against me at the back. My father's eyes were glistening and hard and his breath reeked with liquor. I wondered if he would strike me, and my mind was panic-stricken . . . if he did I would . . . yes, I would get at his throat with my teeth! . . .

We stood staring into each other's eyes, enemies. Then the rope fell from his hand and curled snake-like about his feet. Turning without a word, he walked heavily through the alley-gate, his big shoulders round and stooped . . . so stooped . . . his shirt ragged and dirty . . . he stumbled along the railway track. . . .

How long it took him to vanish around the bend! When he had disappeared, I found my mother lying prostrate across her bed. I stood close beside her and stared at the faded blue calcimined wall. To touch her would have been impossible.

Perhaps when I was a baby I had touched her in affection. But that was years ago and I had forgotten. Now I could not. I turned in silence and went back to the yard. When she came out again, I had nearly finished the washing, and darkness had come.

"No, I'd just as leave finish it ... there ain't much more," I protested when she came near.

A bond had at last been welded between us two ... a bond of misery that was never broken. *Agnes Smedley*

Kalimonje now realized that she could no longer seek answers for all her questions from her mother. For the first time she felt a wall between them. There was a time when the wall was so high that Kalimonje felt completely isolated. But luckily for her the wall became lower—or was it because the house leaned over its edges? She still did not tell her mother anything, but a form of communication that did not need words developed between them. Kalimonje was relieved to realize that even as she crossed from the world where every thought was verbalized to a world where she could not possibly talk about all her thoughts and feelings, concerned spirits still found a meeting-place.

Perhaps it was fortunate for Kalimonje that the first picking of dry beans came. Occupied in picking and carrying the beans home, then drying them and beating them to separate the beans from the pods, she found little time for distracting speculation. After the beans came the harvesting of millet. This was the part of the harvesting process she hated most. It lasted forever, picking up each tiny finger of the millet and cutting it singly. Then came the fermenting time, when the millet

81

would stay in a heap to gain flavor. When they spread it out after a week or two, the heap emitted so much heat and such a strange smell that few could bear the work. But this was the work of women, and a woman must learn to enjoy it. The men helped with the cutting and then the beating to separate the grain from the chaff. The rest of the processing, including the winnowing, was reserved for the womenfolk.

Kalimonje began to resent the kind of life a woman led. Look at her mother. She could hardly remember seeing her just sitting and taking it easy. Drawing water, carrying wood, bringing food home, cooking it. All the preparations, the digging, the children. Everything rested on mother. All that the men did was to sit under a tree and talk, waiting for an invasion so that they might guard the clan's boundaries. In Kalimonje's life there had been no such invasion. It seemed to her a rather lazy way of getting out of work.

"Mama," she once demanded, "why do you slave so?" Her mother looked at her in great surprise.

"Slave? What do you mean?"

"You never have a moment of rest."

"We have to live."

"Why don't the men help?"

Mama shrugged her shoulders and went on winnowing the millet on her straw tray. Kalimonje wasn't going to give up so easily.

"I wish I wasn't born a woman," she said with a sigh.

"Change yourself, dear," her mother suggested with an edge to her voice. To show her disgust, Kalimonje was no longer a keen helper of mother. Why didn't mama complain to the men so that they could help? But as days passed, she went back to her routine of doing almost half the daily chores. She sympathized with her mother, seeing herself soon grinding on that same stone.   *Miriam Khamadi Were*

"It's my dreadful temper! I try to cure it; I think I have, and then it breaks out worse than ever. Oh, Mother, what shall I do? What shall I do?" cried poor Jo, in despair.

"Watch and pray, dear, never get tired of trying, and never think it is impossible to conquer your fault," said Mrs. March, drawing the blowzy head to her shoulder and kissing the wet cheek so tenderly that Jo cried harder than ever.

"You don't know, you can't guess how bad it is! It seems as if I could do anything when I'm in a passion; I get so savage, I could hurt anyone and enjoy it. I'm afraid I *shall* do something dreadful some day, and spoil my life, and make everybody hate me. Oh, Mother, help me, do help me!"

"I will, my child, I will. Don't cry so bitterly, but remember this day, and resolve with all your soul that you will never know another like it. Jo, dear, we all have our temptations, some far greater than yours, and it often takes us all our lives to conquer them. You think your temper is the worst in the world, but mine used to be just like it."

"Yours, Mother? Why, you are never angry!" And for the moment Jo forgot remorse in surprise.

"I've been trying to cure it for forty years, and have only succeeded in controlling it. I am angry nearly every day of my life, Jo, but I have learned not to show it; and I still hope to learn not to feel it, though it may take me another forty years to do so."

The patience and the humility of the face she loved so well was a better lesson to Jo than the wisest lecture, the sharpest reproof. She felt comforted at once by the sympathy and confidence given her; the knowledge that her mother had a fault like hers, and tried to mend it, made her own easier to bear and strengthened her resolution to cure it, though forty years seemed rather a long time to watch and pray to a girl of fifteen.   *Louisa May Alcott*

83

"We'll set awhile. My head is balloony, balloony. Balloony."
She staggered, put her arms around Mazie, sang:

> *O Shenandoah I love thy daughter*
> *I'll bring her safe through stormy water*

smiled so radiantly, Mazie's heart leapt. Arm in arm, they sat
down under the catalpa. That look was on her mother's face
again, her eyes so shining and remote. She began stroking
Mazie's hair in a kind of languor, a swoon. Gently and absently
she stroked.

> *Around the springs of gray my wild root weaves,*
> *Traveler repose and dream among my leaves*

her mother sang. A fragile old remembered comfort streamed
from the stroking fingers into Mazie, gathered to some shy
bliss that shone despairingly over suppurating hurt and want
and fear and shamings—the Harm of years. River wind shim-
mered and burnished the bright grasses, her mother's hand
stroked, stroked. Young catalpa leaves overhead quivered and
glistened, bright reflected light flowed over, 'lumined their
faces. A bee rested on Mazie's leg; magic!—flew away; and a
butterfly wavered near, settled, folded its wings, flew again.

> *I saw a ship a sailing*

her mother sang.

> *A sailing on the sea*

Mazie felt the strange happiness in her mother's body,
happiness that had nought to do with them, with her; happiness
and farness and selfness.

> *I saw a ship a sailing*
> *And on that ship was me.*

The fingers stroked, spun a web, cocooned Mazie into happiness and intactness and selfness. Soft wove the bliss round hurt and fear and want and shame—the old worn fragile bliss, a new frail selfness bliss, healing, transforming. Up from the grasses, from the earth, from the broad tree trunk at their back, latent life streamed and seeded. The air and self shone boundless. Absently, her mother stroked; stroked unfolding, wingedness, boundlessness.

"I'm hungry," Ben said.

"Watch me jump," Jimmie called imperiously. "Momma, Mazie, watch. You're not watching!"

The wind shifted, blew packing house. A tremble of complicity ran through Mazie's body; with both hands she tethered her mother's hand to keep it stroking. Too late. Something whirred, severed, sank. *Between a breath, between a heartbeat, the weight settled, the bounds reclaimed.*

"I'm watching," Anna called. The mother look was back on her face, the mother alertness, attunement, in her bounded body. . . .

Never again, but once, did Mazie see that look—the other look—on her mother's face.   *Tillie Olsen*

APRIL

Deeper than sleep but not so deep as death
I lay there sleeping and my magic head remembered
    and forgot. On first cry I
remembered and forgot and did believe.
I knew love and I knew evil:
woke to the burning song and the tree burning blind,
despair of our days and the calm milk-giver who knows
    sleep, knows growth, the sex of fire and grass,
and the black snake with gold bones.

Black sleeps, gold burns; on second cry I woke
fully and gave to feed and fed on feeding.
Gold seed, green pain, my wizards in the earth
walked through the house, black in the morning dark.
Shadows grew in my veins, my bright belief,
my head of dreams deeper than night and sleep.
Voices of all black animals crying to drink,
cries of all birth arise, simple as we,
found in the leaves, in clouds and dark, in dream,
deep as this hour, ready again to sleep.

Muriel Rukeyser

There are times in life when one does the right thing,

the thing one will not regret,
when the child wakes crying "mama," late
as you are about to close your book and sleep
and she will not be comforted back to her crib,
she points you out of her room, into yours,
you tell her, "I was just reading here in bed,"
she says, "read a book," you explain it's not a children's
   book
but you sit with her anyway, she lays her head on your
   breast,
one-handed, you hold your small book, silently read,
resting it on the bed to turn pages
and she, thumb in mouth, closes her eyes, drifts,
not asleep—when you look down at her, her lids open,
and once you try to carry her back
but she cries, so you return to your bed again and book,
and the way a warmer air will replace a cooler with a slight
shift of wind, or swimming, entering a mild current, you
enter this pleasure, the quiet book, your daughter in your
   lap,
an articulate person now, able to converse, yet still
her cry is for you, her comfort in you,
it is your breast she lays her head upon,
you are lovers, asking nothing but this bodily presence.
She hovers between sleep, you read your book,
you give yourself this hour, sweet and quiet beyond flowers
beyond lilies of the valley and lilacs even, the smell of her
   breath,

the warm damp between her head and your breast. Past
   midnight
she blinks her eyes, wiggles toward a familiar position,
utters one word, "sleeping." You carry her swiftly into her
   crib,
cover her, close the door halfway, and it is this sense of
   rightness,
that something has been healed, something
you will never know, will never have to know.

Ellen Bass

Charlotte watched her daughter cry. She had come home at six forty-five and had spent the rest of the evening crying in her room.

Charlotte had tried to say comforting things like "Anything I can do?" "How about going to the deli with me?" "Want to play some cards?" But those were the wrong things and she knew it. She could only sit in the kitchen, playing games of solitaire and listening to her girl, who lay in a deep misery she could not touch. . . .

Charlotte knocked on the door. "I'm going to hit the hay," she said.

"Okay," Felicitas said, almost silently.

"I was thinking maybe you'd better sleep in the bed with me. I've turned the heat off in your room and it's chilly."

Felicitas sobbed.

"Come on, bean," said Charlotte.

They got into the old hard bed with the metal headboard and the horsehair mattress that had been Charlotte's mother's. Charlotte lay down, said goodnight, kissed her daughter and turned her back to her. Felicitas slipped in behind her mother like a spoon. Exhausted from a day of crying, she fell instantly asleep. Charlotte lay awake and thought of mothers who killed the men who hurt their daughters. Only she did not know who to kill and why she had to kill him. And her child was not a child.   *Mary Gordon*

It is six-thirty and the little room is very cold. Janet's window is ... streaming with grey wet. I light the gas fire, while she sits up in bed, surrounded by bright patches of color from her comics, watching me to see if I do everything as usual, and reading at the same time. ... A train passes, and the walls shake slightly. I go over to kiss her, and smell the good smell of warm flesh, and hair, and the stuff of her pyjamas, heated by sleep. While her room warms I go into the kitchen and prepare her breakfast—cereal, fried eggs and tea, on a tray. I take the tray back into her room, and she eats her breakfast sitting up in bed, and I drink tea and smoke. The house is dead still. ... Through the wall, a baby is crying. It gives me a feeling of continuity, of rest, the baby crying, as Janet once cried. It is the contented half-sleepy cry of a baby who has been fed and will be asleep in a moment. Janet says: "Why don't we have another baby?" She says this often. And I say: "Because I haven't got a husband and you must have a husband to get a baby." ... Now the room is warm, and she gets out of bed in her white sleeping suit, looking fragile and vulnerable. She puts her arms around my neck and swings on it, back and forth, singing: Rockabye baby. I swing her and sing—babying her, she has become the baby next door, the baby I won't have. Then, abruptly, she lets me go, so tht I feel myself spring up like a tree that has been bent over by a weight. She dressed herself, crooning, still half-drowsy, still peaceful. I think that she will retain the peace for years, until the pressure comes on her, and she must start thinking. ... I want very much to protect her from the pressure, to postpone it; then I tell myself I must protect her from nothing, this need is really Anna wanting to protect Anna. ... The baby is asleep next door; there is the silence of content from the baby. Everyone asleep save me and Janet. It is a feeling of intimacy and exclusiveness—

90

a feeling that began when she was born, when she and I were awake together at times when the city slept around us. It is a warm, lazy, intimate gaiety. She seems to me so fragile that I want to put out my hand to save her from a wrong step, or a careless movement; and at the same time so strong that she is immortal. I feel ... a need to laugh out in triumph, because of this marvellous, precarious, immortal human being, in spite of the weight of death.   *Doris Lessing*

1

2

3

4

5

6

7

8

9

10

11

12

13

14

15

16

17

18

19

20

21

22

23

24

25

26

27

28

29

30

MAY
Mothering:
Some Troublous
Contexts
Then–Yet–and Now

"Who's to care about them if we don't, who?"
                                        Tillie Olsen

NASON
Martha Jane   Oct. 6, 1841   2 yrs.
Charles   Feb. 11, 1846   9 yrs. 2 mos.
Lowell
Lizzie Bell
Little Goldie
Thaddeus
TOO PURE FOR EARTH
Putney, Vermont

ANNIE ROSE
1867   1873
She was but 5 years, 20 days old
CALLED TO JOIN HER BROTHERS AND HER SISTERS
WHERE PARTING IS NEVER MORE
YOU HAVE THEM ALL NOW, LORD
Arlington, Massachusetts

MILENA WILETT
1 yr. old
Thy Mother strives in patient trust
Her bleeding heart to bow
For safe in God, the Good, the Just
Her baby's sleeping now
Fort Bragg, California

1884
OUR MOTHER CHARITY
And Baby
Jennie, Tryphena, and Little Henry too
Sweet Rest
Our Mother, In Whose Love We Were So Blest
St. Paul, Minnesota

MILENA ROSARIO
1894   1930
Beloved Mother of Eleven, Wife and Sister Dear

She suffered so, Lord she has had her Hell
Now in Heaven with Jesus, she does surely dwell

Sweet rest at last.
Colma, California

July 26. At last it is over, and our dear little one is gone from us.... My Charley—my beautiful, loving gladsome baby, so loving, so sweet, so full of life and hope and strength—now lies shrouded, pale and cold in the room below.... He has been my pride and joy. Many a heartache has he cured for me. Many an anxious night have I held him to my bosom and felt the sorrow and loneliness pass out of me with the touch of his little warm hands. Yet I have just seen him in his death agony, looked on his imploring face when I could not help nor soothe nor do one thing, not one, to mitigate his cruel suffering, do nothing but pray in my anguish that he might die soon. I write as though there were no sorrow like my sorrow.

Harriet Beecher Stowe, who
"spent many a night weeping,
the [new] baby sleeping beside
me as I thought of the slave
mothers whose babes were torn
from them."

"[I took] some thin boards that had been laid down to step on, to keep the mud out of the house. Brother John cut them out the proper shape for a little casket and tacked them together, and I covered them with the black broadcloth. I lined the box with cotton batting, tacking it neatly in the corners. I had an old white dress of thin stuff. I folded it in pleats and tacked it over the batting. I covered a board for the top in the same way. Brother had some pretty little white tacks that looked like silver. I tacked them in around the edge like a finish. And then I made a pillow of the white stuff and laid the baby on it. Brother John wept, and said: "My! Sister! What *can't* you do?" ... We buried the little baby on our farm.

"Whatever the work to be carried through to completion, whether for the dead or the living, one's children must not be neglected. Gus used to follow me around sometimes, those first years on the farm, saying doggedly: 'Mother! Mother! I've got me some tiredness, I want to be took.' ...

"It seemed as if the only time when I felt justified in taking up a book or paper was when I sat down to nurse my babies. I always nursed them till they were pretty big. I couldn't bear to wean them—they kept so fat and pretty as long as I fed them at the breast.... Anyway, for many years all my household tasks were performed with an ear cocked for the cry of a waking baby. How often I used to think: 'What happiness it would be if I had nothing to do *except* take care of my babies!' There was one terrible period when, for two years, I carried my little sick Carrie around with me on a pillow as I went from stove to table or from room to room, doing my work.

"Such a way of living is hard, *hard*, HARD."

Harriet Connor Brown

"Olivia," she began timidly at last, "aren't you ever going to have any more children?"

"Oh, I hope so, Mother. I haven't been strong, you know, since the first one. We didn't think it advisable."

"Well, if you can manage it that way . . ." There was a trace in her tone of the woman who hadn't been able to manage. I wished to reassure her.

"When I was in the hospital the doctor told me . . ." I could see the deep flush rising over her face and neck; there were some things which her generation had never faced. I let them fall with her hands and sat gazing at the red core of the base burner, waiting until she should take up her thought again.

"I used to think those things weren't right, Olivia, but I don't know. Sometimes I think it isn't right, either, to bring them into the world when there is no welcome for them." She struggled with the admission. "You and I, Olivia, we never got on together."

"But that's all past now, Mother." She clung to me for a while for reassurance.

"I hope so, I hope so; but still there are things I've always wanted to tell you. When you wrote me about going on the stage . . . there are wild things in you, Olivia, things I never looked for in a daughter of mine, things I can't understand nor account for unless—unless it was I turned you against life . . . my kind of life . . . before you were born. Many's the time I've seen you hating it and I've been harsh with you; but I wanted you should know I was being harsh with myself . . ."

"Mother, dear, is it good for you to talk so?"

"Yes, yes, I've wanted to. You see it was after your father came home from the war and we were all broken up. Forester was sickly, and there was the one that died. So when I knew you were coming, I—hated you, Olivia. I wanted things

103

different. I hated you ... until I heard you cry. You cried all the time when you were little, Olivia, and it was I that was crying in you.

Mary Austin

As Judith sat by the bedside of the sick child that she had begrudged the life before it was born, her heart failed her at the thought that the little one might die. . . .

And yet at the same moment that she yearned over the sick child, another set of thoughts, strange and sinister, came . . . thoughts that had come to her at other times and before which she had quailed, as, in the darkness of a wakeful night, one quails before thoughts of approaching death.

Of what use after all that this baby should live? She would live only to endure, to be patient, to work, to suffer; and at last, when she had gone through all these things, to die without ever having lived and without knowing that she had never lived. Judith had seen grow up in the families of the neighbors and among her own kin dozens of just such little girls ... [to pass] quickly from that into ... the ... burdens of too frequent maternity. . . .

Sitting by the sick child through the long vigils ... the mother dwelt upon these thoughts. ... And following them out to the end they brought her relentlessly to the conclusion that it would be better that the child should die. . . . No, she could not have her baby die. She must not die. . . . The mother shrank and quailed, feeling her burden greater than she could bear.

Edith Summers Kelley

Gertie spent long hours over the ironing and the tedious housework, trying to think up words for a letter [to her runaway son]—a letter that would make him understand she loved him. Then, unable to put the words together, she would think past a perfect letter, written. Suppose he knew she loved him; as Enoch would have said, "So what?" Her love had ever been a burden, laying on him false hopes that, dead, weighed down still more the burden of his misery.

She missed him, but could never tell him how she missed him most. She hated herself when she lied, trying to make herself believe she missed him the way a mother ought to miss a child. In the old song ballads mothers cried, looking at tables with empty plates and rooms with empty beds. But how could a body weep over a table where, even with one gone, there was yet hardly room for those remaining. The gas pipes were still overcrowded with drying clothes; and eight quarts of milk instead of ten in the Icy Heart meant only less crowding, not vacant space. Two pounds of hamburger cost less than two and a half, and— She would hate herself for thinking of the money saved, and try never to think that living was easier with no child sleeping in the little living room.   *Harriette Arnow*

... and then the whine that always hurt: "We're the onliest ones ain't got none."   *Harriette Arnow*

Before morning, Nnu Ego had her second set of twins, which Nnaife delivered, as he sat on the upturned mortar which they had brought from the kitchen. Okpo was there to help with hot water, knives and things. Nnaife was not very pleased with the outcome: all this ballyhoo for two more girls! If one had to have twins, why girls, for Olisa's sake?

The arrival of her new twin daughters had a subduing effect upon Nnu Ego. She felt more inadequate than ever. Men—all they were interested in were male babies to keep their names going. But did not a woman have to bear the woman-child who would later bear the sons? "God, when will you create a woman who will be fulfilled in herself, a full human being, not anybody's appendage?" she prayed desperately. "After all, I was born alone, and I shall die alone. What have I gained from all this? Yes, I have many children, but what do I have to feed them on? On my life. I have to work myself to the bone to look after them, I have to give them my all. And if I am lucky enough to die in peace, I even have to give them my soul. They will worship my dead spirit to provide for them: it will be hailed as a good spirit so long as there are plenty of yams and children in the family, but if anything should go wrong, if a young wife does not conceive or there is a famine, my dead spirit will be blamed. When will I be free?"

But even in her confusion she knew the answer: "Never, not even in death. I am a prisoner of my own flesh and blood. Is it such an enviable position? The men make it look as if we must aspire for children or die. That's why when I lost my first son I wanted to die, because I failed to live up to the standard expected of me by the males in my life, my father and my husband—and now I have to include my sons. But who made the law that we should not hope in our daughters? ...

The two baby girls were given the names Obiageli, meaning

"She who has come to enjoy wealth," and Malachi, meaning "You do not know what tomorrow will bring."

Buchi Emecheta

Pregnancy was a chronic condition. . . . Suggestions as to what to do for a girl who was "in trouble" or a married woman who was "caught" passed from mouth to mouth—herb teas, turpentine, steaming, rolling downstairs, inserting slippery elm, knitting needles, shoe-hooks. . . . The doomed women implored me to reveal the "secret" rich people had, offering to pay me extra to tell them; many really believed I was holding back information for money. They asked everybody and tried anything, but nothing did them any good. On Saturday nights I have seen groups of from fifty to one hundred with their shawls over their heads waiting outside the office of a five-dollar abortionist. . . . I knew the women personally. They were living, breathing, human beings, with hopes, fears, and aspirations like my own, yet their weary, misshapen bodies, "always ailing, never failing," were destined to be thrown on the scrap heap before they were thirty-five. I could not escape from the facts of their wretchedness; neither was I able to see any way out. . . .

Then one stifling mid-July day of 1912 I was summoned to a Grand Street tenement. . . . Jake Sachs, a truck driver scarcely older than his wife, had come home to find the three children crying and her unconscious from the effects of a self-induced abortion. . . .

At the end of three weeks, as I was preparing to leave the fragile patient to take up her difficult life once more, she finally voiced her fears, "Another baby will finish me, I suppose?"

"It's too early to talk about that," I temporized.

But when the doctor came to make his last call, I drew him aside. "Mrs. Sachs is terribly worried about having another baby."

"She well may be," replied the doctor, and then he stood before her and said, "Any more such capers, young woman, and there'll be no need to send for me."

"I know, doctor," she replied timidly, "but," and she hesitated as though it took all her courage to say it, "what can I do to prevent it?" . . . Picking up his hat and bag to depart [the doctor] said, "Tell Jake to sleep on the roof."

. . . Even through my sudden tears I could see stamped on her face an expression of absolute despair. We simply looked at each other, saying no word until the door had closed behind the doctor. Then she lifted her thin, blue-veined hands and clasped them beseechingly. "He can't understand. He's only a man. But you do, don't you? Please tell me the secret, and I'll never breathe it to a soul. *Please!*" . . . I really did not know what to say to her or how to convince her of my own ignorance; I was helpless. . . .

The telephone rang one evening three months later, and John Sachs' agitated voice begged me to come at once; his wife was sick again and from the same cause. . . .

Mrs. Sachs was in a coma and died within ten minutes. I folded her still hands across her breast, remembering how they had pleaded with me, begging so humbly for the knowledge which was her right. . . . I . . . resolved to seek out the root of evil, to do something to change the destiny of mothers whose miseries were vast as the sky.   *Margaret Sanger*

EVERY Mother Is a Working Woman.
                                        Button Slogan

Why couldn't they just stay like this—so soft and easy to care for? How she had loved them this way. Taking the baby's hand in her mouth, she sucked at the small fingers and watched it giggle and try to reach for her nose. She poked her thumb into the dimpled cheek and lifted the child onto her breast so she could stroke its finely curled hair and inhale the mingled sweetness of mineral oil and talcum powder that lay in the creases of its neck. Oh, for them to stay like this, when they could be fed from her body so there were no welfare offices to sit in all day or food stamp lines to stand on, when she alone could be their substance and their world, when there were no neighbors or teachers or social workers to answer to about their actions. They stayed where you put them and were so easy to keep clean.

She'd spend hours washing, pressing, and folding the miniature clothes, blankets, and sheets. The left-handed corner of her bedroom which held the white wooden crib and dresser was dusted and mopped religiously. . . . That brown body . . . was bathed and oiled twice a day . . . the pastel flannel and percales . . . personally scrubbed and sterilized . . . the hair brushes . . . boiled each week and replaced each month.

Gloria Naylor

She was a beautiful baby. She blew shining bubbles of sound. She loved motion, loved light, loved color and music and textures. She would lie on the floor in her blue overalls patting the surface so hard in ecstasy her hands and feet would blur. She was a miracle to me, but when she was eight months old I had to leave her daytimes with the woman downstairs to whom she was no miracle at all, for I worked or looked for work and for Emily's father, who "could no longer endure" (he wrote in his goodbye note) "sharing want with us."

I was nineteen. ... I would start running as soon as I got off the streetcar, running up the stairs, the place smelling sour, and awake or asleep to startle awake, when she saw me she would break into a clogged weeping that could not be comforted, a weeping I can hear yet.

After a while I found a job hashing at night so I could be with her days, and it was better. But it came to where I had to bring her to his family and leave her.

It took a long time to raise the money for her fare back. Then she got chicken pox and I had to wait longer. When she finally came, I hardly knew her. ... All the baby loveliness gone.

She was two. Old enough for nursery school they said, and I did not know then what I know now—the fatigue of the long day, and the lacerations of group life in the kinds of nurseries that are only parking places for children.

Except that it would have made no difference if I had known. It was the only place there was. It was the only way we could be together, the only way I could hold a job.

And even without knowing, I knew.

Tillie Olsen

110

Your clear eye is the one absolutely beautiful thing.
I want to fill it with color and ducks.
The zoo of the new

Whose names you meditate—
April snowdrop, Indian pipe,
Little

Stalk without wrinkle,
Pool in which images
Should be grand and classical

Not this troublous
Wringing of hands, this dark
Ceiling without a star.

Sylvia Plath

Sue asked, why is there a line
between your eyes, why
are your eyebrows

hunched? We were having lunch
in a Chinese restaurant. I felt hunted.
There were many things not

done, they might never be
done, the bills were not
paid, I had almost forgotten

the nursery school car pool, old food
in the refrigerator was
rotting, poisonous: so thin

are the wires holding
me I sleep
all the time. Shadows

hover. They might take the shape of birds
or policemen. We were illegally
parked. I am wrongfully

alive, presumed
free. And my daughter, five, who had
been laughing, saw

the shadows, hers.

Patricia Cumming

I knew I was going to have to talk to the children about their father's absence. Not knowing how to do it, I waited.

Anna came in from summer play and watched me put my kitchen shelves in order. She asked me if Daddy was just waiting for the house to be cleaned before coming home.

"I'll answer that at lunch," I said. "Go get your brother." I was in a countdown for time. I didn't want to injure their idea of their father, but yet wanted to let them know he wouldn't be living with us.

I leaned against the counter watching the children from the perspective of their youth and vulnerability. Mary Elisabeth lifted the high-chair tray and dropped it to watch her bread crust jump. Matthew was rotating his sandwich in his hand, trying to turn the square bread into a wheel by controlled bites.

I took a breath and said, "Your father loves you very much, even though he has gone to live at another's house." I thought if we could see this sentence in the air, it would arc like an expression of grief over us.

Anna had only one thing to say: "I had hoped he would choose us." I chased her statement with three bowls, filling each one with too much ice cream.

I took them to the park and pushed them on the swings higher and harder than I ever had before.   *Laurel Lee*

113

She recognizes miner's lettuce
nibbles its round leaf.
Her father asks *Do you know
not to eat the other plants?*
and she nods solemnly.
We have taught her not to swallow pits
of cherries or olives.
She spits them out bald
and repeats *Could make a child sick.*
And walking, when we hear a car
she runs to the side of the road
stands, stationary, until it passes.
But how do I protect her
from men who rape children?
from poison in the air?
from nuclear holocaust?

Ellen Bass

She is coming. She runs up the stairs two at a time with her light graceful step, and I know she is happy tonight. Whatever it was that occasioned your call did not happen today.

"Aren't you ever going to finish the ironing, Mother? Whistler painted his mother in a rocker. I'd have to paint mine standing over an ironing board." This is one of her communicative nights and she tells me everything and nothing as she fixes herself a plate of food out of the icebox.

She is so lovely. Why did you want me to come in at all? Why were you concerned? She will find her way.

She starts up the stairs to bed. "Don't get me up with the rest in the morning." "But I thought you were having midterms." "Oh, those," she come back in, kisses me, and says quite lightly, "in a couple of years when we'll all be atom-dead they won't matter a bit."

She has said it before. She *believes* it. But because I have been dredging the past, and all that compounds a human being is so heavy and meaningful in me, I cannot endure it tonight. . . .

Let her be. So all that is in her will not bloom—but in how many does it? There is still enough left to live by. Only help her to know—help make it so there is cause for her to know—that she is more than this dress on the ironing board, helpless before the iron.

Tillie Olsen

1

2

3

4

5

6

7

8

9

10

11

12

13

14

15

16

17

18

19

20

21

22

23

24

25

26

27

28

29

30

31

JUNE
Mothering: Some Extremities and Meditations

"Look. . . . At what price we buy life."
Bryna Bar Oni

The mother's battle for her child . . . needs to become a common human battle, waged in love and in the passion for survival.   *Adrienne Rich*

That night ... the last torment was inflicted on the dying child in the shape of a monstrous hiccough. It started from far, far down, shot out with the violence of an explosion, and seemed as if it would tear the little body in two. Under this new blow Mary's courage all but failed her. In vain did Mahony, his arm round her bent shoulders, try to soothe her. "My darling, it sounds worse than it is. We feel it more than she does ... now." Each time it burst forth an irrepressible shudder ran through Mary, as if it were she herself who was being racked.— And on this night her passionate prayer ran: "Take her, God! ... take her if you must! I give her back to you. But oh, let it be soon! ... stop her suffering ... give her peace." And as hour after hour dragged by, without respite, she rounded on Him and fiercely upbraided Him. "It is cruel of You ... cruel! No earthly father would torture a child as You are doing. ... You, all-powerful, and called Love!"

But, little by little, so stealthily that its coming was imperceptible, the ultimate peace fell: by daybreak there was nothing more to hope or to fear. Throughout the long day that followed—it seemed made of years, yet passed like an hour— Lallie lay in coma, drawing breaths that were part snores, part heavy sighs. Time and place ceased to exist for Mary, as she sat and watched her child die. Through noon and afternoon, and on into the dark, she tirelessly wiped the damp brow and matted curls, fanned off the greedy flies, one little inert hand held firmly in her own: perhaps somehow, on this, her darling's last, fearsome journey, the single journey in her short life that she had taken unattended, something would tell her that her mother was with her, her mother's love keeping and holding her.—On this day Richard did not leave the house. And their kind friend again fetched away the other children.

123

The *other* children? ... what need now of this word! Henceforth, there would always and for ever be only two. Never again, if not by accident, would the proud words, "My three!" cross her lips.—There she sat, committing to oblivion her mother-store of fond and foolish dreams, the lovely fabric of hopes and plans that she had woven about this little dear one's future; sat bidding farewell to many a tiny endearing feature of which none but she knew: in this spun-glass hair the one rebellious curl that would not twist with the rest; secret dimples kneaded in the baby body; the tiny birthmark below the right shoulder; the chubby, dimpled hands ... all now destined to be shut away and hidden from sight. Oh, what was the use of creating so fair a thing, merely to destroy it! (They say He knows all, but never, never can He have known what it means to be a mother.)

Henry Handel (Ethel Florence) Richardson

Abortions will not let you forget.
You remember the children you got that you did
    not get,
The damp small pulps with a little or with no hair,
The singers and workers that never handled the
    air. . . .

I have heard in the voices of the wind the voices
    of my dim killed children.
I have contracted. I have eased
My dim dears at the breasts they could never suck.
I have said, Sweets, if I sinned, if I seized
Your luck
And your lives from you unfinished reach,
If I stole your births and your names,
Your straight baby tears and your games,
Your stilted or lovely loves, your tumults, your
    marriages, aches, and your deaths,
If I poisoned the beginnings of your breaths,
Believe that even in my deliberateness I was not
    deliberate.

Believe me, I loved you all.
Believe me, I knew you, though faintly, and I
    loved, I loved you
All.

Gwendolyn Brooks

1890 ... It has been two days since they came and took the children away. My body is greatly chilled. All our blankets have been used to bring me warmth. The women keep the fire blazing. The men sit. They talk among themselves. We are frightened by this sudden child-stealing. We signed papers, the agent said. This gave them rights to take our babies. It is good for them, the agent said. I do not know civilized. I hold myself tight in fear of flying apart into the air. The others try to feed me. Can they feed a dead woman? I have stopped talking. When my mouth opens, only air escapes. I have used up my sound screaming their names ... She sees Deer! Walking Fox! My eyes stare at the room, the walls of scrubbed wood, the floor of dirt. I know there are People here, but I cannot see them. I see a darkness, like the lake at New Moon, black, unmoving. In the center, a picture of my son and daughter being lifted onto the train. My daughter wearing the dark blue, heavy dress. All of the girls dressed alike. Her hair covered by a strange basket tied under her chin. Never have I seen such eyes! They burn into my head even now. ... So many children crying, screaming. The sun on our bodies, our heads. The train screeching like a crow, sounding like laughter. Smoke and dirt pumping out of the insides of the train. So many People. So many children. The women, standing as if in prayer, our hands lifted, reaching. The dust sifting down on our palms. Our palms making motions at the sky. Our fingers closing like the claws of the bear. I see this now. ... No sounds of children playing games and laughing. Even the dogs have ceased their noises. They lay outside each doorway, waiting. I hear this. The voices of children. They cry. They pray. They call me. ... Nisten ha. I hear this. Nisten ha.

Beth Brant

1978 ... I am awakened by the dream. In the dream, my daughter is dead. Her father is returning her body to me in pieces. He keeps her heart. I thought I screamed ... Patricia! I sit up in bed, swallowing air as if for nourishment. The dream remains in the air. I rise to go to her room. Ellen tries to lead me back to bed, but I have to see once again. I open her door ... she is gone. The room empty, lonely. They said it was in her best interests. How can it be? She is only six, a baby who needs her mothers. She loves us. This is not happening. I will not believe this. Oh god, I think I have died. Night after night, Ellen holds me as I shake. Our sobs stifling the air in our room. We lie in our bed and try to give comfort. My mind can't think beyond last week when she left. I would have killed him if I'd had the chance. He took her hand and pulled her to the car. The look in his eyes of triumph. It was a contest to him. I know he will teach her to hate us. He will! I see her dear face. Her face looking out the back window of his car. Her mouth forming the word over and over ... Mommy Mama. Her dark braids tied with red yarn. Her front teeth missing. Her overalls with the yellow flower on the pocket, embroidered by Ellen's hands. So lovingly she sewed the yellow wool. Patricia waiting quietly until she was finished. Ellen promising to teach her the designs ... chain stitch, french knot, split stitch. How Patricia told everyone that Ellen made the flower just for her. So proud of her overalls. I open the closet door. Almost everything is gone. A few little things hang there limp, abandoned. I pull a blue dress from a hanger and take it back to my room. Ellen tries to take it away from me, but I hold on, the soft, blue cotton smelling like her. How is it possible to feel such pain and live? Ellen?! She croons my name ... Mary ... Mary ... I love you. She sings me to sleep.

Beth Brant

As we lay flat beneath the foliage of the fallen trees, we saw partisans from a neighboring group running past, some of them wounded. It was the first group to be attacked: only 250 people to fight against thousands of Germans equipped with tanks and armed with machine guns and grenades.

[My sister] Yentl and her two children were overcome with fatigue. Rochele, the six-year-old, clung to her mother and cried that she was cold, wet and hungry. The infant, Matys, clung tightly to Yentl's dry breasts, sucking pus from her boils instead of milk.

Rochele had lost her shoes running through the woods and had cut her feet on the thorns. I took off my high-laced shoes and gave them to her to protect her soft feet as much as possible from the wild overgrown burdock and bramble. I was overcome with pain as I looked at my family, but I tried to comfort them: "Tomorrow it will quiet down; we'll go back to our camp and find food then." But all the while we smelled the smoke of our burning tents and huts. . . .

The weather was exceptionally hot and dry. Fear made us forget our hunger, but we could not overcome the parched feeling of our dry mouths. We were slowly dehydrating. The children cried with the last strength they possessed. Hearing their cries, the Germans stepped up their shooting and shouted, "Halt!" Seryosha, who had taken such devoted care of the babies and the small children, asked the mothers with infants to leave the rest of the group because they jeopardized the survival of all of us.

Yentl and her son joined five other women and their small children. They walked to a secluded area to stay overnight. Rochele did not want her mother to go and started to cry. I embraced her tightly and tried to assure her that next day we would all be together again.

The next morning, Sunday, the mothers came back to us carrying dead children. My sister was the only one whose baby was still alive. Rochele kissed and hugged her mother, but the reunion was not a joyful one. Yentl, her face the color of ash, lay bare the woes of the scene she had witnessed the night before.

"We couldn't keep our children quiet. They felt our fear and our restlessness. The woods have a language of their own, and every murmur of the leaves, every sound of a squirrel running in the trees made us panic. We were sure the enemy had found us. Suddenly Golda, who was sick and distraught over losing her husband, began wrapping her child with her shawl. With a terrible blank look on her face, she choked her baby to death. The rest of the mothers tried to stop her, but then something happened: they, too, became engulfed in some unexplainable madness ... and began to choke their babies to death.

"I stood there confused. Was I dreaming all this? Or was I witnessing a madness beyond my comprehension?" She paused in her recital, then added softly, "Look at them, Bryna. At what price we buy life."

Six months later my worst fears were realized. ... Along the roadside ... in a pile [of] seven skeletons I recognized Yentl by the half-rotted fur collar on her coat. Only one of her legs still had flesh. My little niece I recognized by the high-laced shoes I had given her. It looked as if all seven people had been caught alive and burned in the bonfire ... [Through it all] even though she was physically exhausted and distraught over the loss of her son, Yentl did retain presence of mind to hold on to her daughter.

Bryna Bar Oni

JUNE

We went home from the hospital, you and I, to a third-floor flat on the backside of a tall dark building. ... You nursed, pulled and sucked, always faster than I created milk. The clinic nurse said, "Give her bottles," and "Rice cereal now, wheat cereal next week." I obeyed, but went on nursing because I could not bear to give up our joining. You smiled, reached, rolled, sat—and couldn't sleep, and did not sleep. And woke every other hour around the clock, day and night, for four long months, and slept only two hours at a time for the next six.

I do not know how I survived that sleepless time. I would play records like "The Great Mandala" and hallucinate the visions on a wall. I moved with constant aching bones, could stand no closed doors or shut-in spaces, lost track of days or weeks and wrote long lists of things to do—which turned out to be, on later reading, totally unintelligible.

It wasn't colic that woke you, frantic, day and night and night and day. But croup and bronchitis and your very own lungs—fighting for breath and air. I'd steam you and hold you and pace the floors and helpless, listen, as you gasped for life. ... The months of nonsleep were deep inside me ... I had fallen asleep to dreams of caring and walking with you—when the dream became real and I heard your sobs and forced myself to rise again.

"Child that I love, do not cry anymore. I cannot stand it any longer. I have to sleep. This house is dark and empty-sounding and your calls echo off the walls and through my eardrums. Do not cry. Do not cry anymore. I will begin to scream and drown you out if you keep on crying. Please go to sleep, do not cry."

I stumble towards your room and switch on the low lamp so the light will not startle you. You toss your body back and

130

forth, arch your back and wail. Trembling, I walk to your bed and check your diaper. I try to speak, to soothe, to give voice to my presence, but my throat constricts in silent screaming and I find I cannot touch your tangled blankets. I force myself to turn and walk away and lean against the door jamb. My knees buckle beneath me and I find myself huddled on the floor. "Please do not cry. Oh child I love, please do not cry. Tonight you can breathe, so let me breathe." I picture myself walking toward you, lifting your tininess in both my hands and flinging you at the window. Mixed with my choking I can hear the glass as it would smash and I see your body, your perfect body, swirl through the air and land three stories below on the pavement.

I begin to vomit. Force myself to my feet as my stomach empties, then, suddenly calm, walk mechanically and still silently to your bed. I change your diaper while you thrash and cry. Go to the kitchen and heat a bottle, carry it in and prop it on a pillow. Slowly, at last, you quiet, although your body still quivers in spasms and shocks. I leave your room, close the door. The largest chair I can find is in the front room and I push it heavily across the hall and up against your door. Shivering, I walk to the hall door, prop it open and descend the stairs, three flights. I open the door to the night fog, and sit, shaking. I had wanted to kill you.

Child of life, child of love. I do not remember how those hours passed. I know that toward morning I wrapped you carefully in blankets and carried you down the stairs and rode a bus, from one end of the city to another. Thinking you would be safe with me if we were not alone. Riding the bus until it was light. Forcing my head to stay upright on my neck, cradling your head on the softness of my arm.

Julie Olsen Edwards

131

Why discourage women from the colossal swallowing up which is the essence of all motherhood, the mad love (for it is there, the love of a mother for her child), and the madness that maternity represents? For her to feel like a man, free from the consequences of maternity, from the fantastic shackles that it implies? That is probably the reason. But if I answer that men are sick precisely because of this, because they do not have the only opportunity offered a human being to experience a bursting of the ego, how would I be answered? That it was man who made motherhood the monstrous burden it is for sure. But to me the historical reasons for the burden and the drudgery seem the most superficial, because for those there is a remedy. And even if men are responsible for this enslaving form of motherhood, is this enough to condemn maternity itself?

Marguerite Duras

one hesitates to bring a child into this world without fixing it up a little. paint a special room. stop sexism. learn how to love. vow to do it better than it was done when you were a baby. vow to make, if necessary, *new* mistakes. vow to be awake for the birth. to believe in joy even in the midst of unbearable pain.

to bear a child. to bare oneself to that experience. to touch a being with love that hasnt done a damn thing to earn your love. to learn how to love. to care for when it cant take care of you when you're sick. to step out of yourself & learn to step back into yourself. this is the second step, the one we, as women, are just learning. to love without giving oneself away. to stand up without being sat back down.

to watch how the children do it, & to let them love us. to realize ourselves in a reciprocal world.   *Alta*

JUNE

The mother is at the open window. She calls the child home. She's a fat lady. She leans forward, supporting herself on her elbows. Her breasts are shoved up under her chin. Her arms are broad and heavy.

I am not the child. She isn't my mother. Still, in my head where remembering is organized for significance (not usefulness), she leans far out. She looks up and down the block. The technical name of this first seeing is "imprint." It often results in life-long love. I play in the street, she stands in the window. I wanted her to call me home to the dark mysterious apartment behind her back, where the father was already eating and the others sat at the kitchen table and waited for the child.

She was destined, with her meaty bossiness, her sighs, her suffering, to be dumped into the villain room of social meaning and psychological causation. When this happened to her she had just touched the first rung of the great American immigrant ladder. Her husband was ahead of her, her intentional bulk kept him from slipping. Their children were a couple of rungs above them. She believed she would follow them up into the English language, education and respect.

Unfortunately, science and literature had turned against her. What use was my accumulating affection when the brains of the opposition included her son the doctor and her son the novelist? Because of them, she never even had a chance at the crown of apple pie awarded her American-born sisters and accepted by them when they agreed to give up their powerful pioneer dispositions.

What is wrong with the world? the growing person might have asked. The year was 1932 or perhaps 1942. Despite the world-wide fame of those years, the chief investigator into human pain is looking into his own book of awful prognoses. He looks up. Your mother, probably, he says.

134

As for me, I was not paying attention. I missed the mocking campaign.

Of which fifty years have passed, much to my surprise. Using up the days and nights in a lively manner, I have come to the present, daughter of mothers and mother to a couple of grown-up people. They have left home. What have I forgotten to tell? I have told them to be kind. Why? Because my mother was. I have told them when they drop a nickel (or even a shirt) to leave it for the gleaners. It says so in the Bible and I like the idea. Have I told them to always fight for mass transportation and not depend on the auto? Well, they know that. Like all decent kids of Socialist extraction, they can spot the oppressor smiling among the oppressed. Take joy in the struggle against that person, that class, that fact. It's very good for the circulation; I'm sure I said that. Be brave, be truthful, but do they know friendship first, competition second, as the Chinese say? I did say better have a trade, you must know something to be sure of when times are hard, you don't know what the Depression was like, you've had it easy. I've told them everything that was said *to* me or *near* me. As for the rest, there is ordinary place and terrible time—aunts, grandparents, neighbors, all my pals from the job, the playground and the P.T.A. It is on the occasion of their one hundred thousandth bicentennial that I have recalled all those other mothers and their histories.

Grace Paley

What is astonishing, what can give us enormous hope and belief in a future in which the lives of women and children shall be amended and rewoven by women's hands, is all that we have managed to salvage, of ourselves, for our children ... the tenderness, the passion, the trust in our instincts, the evocation of a courage we did not know we owned, the detailed apprehension of another human existence, the full realization of the cost and precariousness of life. The mother's battle for her child—with sickness, with poverty, with war, with all the forces of exploitation and callousness that cheapen human life—needs to become a common human battle, waged in love and in the passion for survival.   *Adrienne Rich*

1

2

3

4

5

6

7

8

9

10

11

12

13

14

15

16

17

18

19

20

21

22

23

24

25

26

27

28

29

30

JULY
Portraits of Mothers: In Love and Sometimes Anguish

She was so fond of every bird and flower, and so full of pity for every grief.   *Emily Dickinson*

Redeemer of waste, champion of leftovers, saviour of nonbiodegradeables, apostle of continuous creation, she has this hunger to find and establish new relations between things, and so create new things .... Nothing is wasted, nothing is cast aside to lead a used up, fragmented, uncreative existence. Everything is suggestive; everything is potentially a part of something else.   *Adele Wiseman*

She was the light and not the lamp.
                    Jessamyn West

Confined to her village by her two successive husbands and four children, she had the power of conjuring up everywhere unexpected crises, burgeonings, metamorphoses, and dramatic miracles, which she herself provoked and whose value she savored to the full . . . . Her form of inconstancy was to fly from the bee to the mouse, from a newborn child to a tree, from a poor person to a poorer, from laughter to torment! How pure are those who lavish themselves in this way! *Colette*

Except on special occasions of "dressing up" or "going out," Mama did not think that she had a visible exterior. She herself lost awareness of that exterior. When lit up like a bonfire with compassion, gaiety, excitement, anger, she was unaware of straggling hair, uneven hemlines, or the old napkin she had grabbed to use as a handkerchief. She was what she felt. She was the light and not the lamp. *Jessamyn West*

Once in Ballardvale, she was away for some weeks. No one knew where she had gone. Then suddenly she came back, thinner and, as I remember, in totally different (and shabby) clothes. She had a complete look of sorrow and of contrition in her eyes. Her eyes were humble; they asked you to forgive her. We forgave her instantly. She went about the house humbly and called us humbly by our names. She called (as she so rarely did) my father by his name. She swept and cleaned and changed the paper on the kitchen shelves. Then, after some days, she opened the piano and played and sang. And we (my brother and myself) sang with her . . . .

A terrible, unhappy, lost, spoiled, bad-tempered child. A

tender, contrite woman, with, somewhere in her blood, the rake's recklessness, the baffled artist's despair . . . . [She] used to use the salt box as an index of time. "What will happen before it is used up?" What *did* happen—to her? I shall never know.
Louise Bogan

My mother never recovered from the death of this child. She had watched her too anxiously through her illness, and her life was a slender stem that would not bear more than one blow from the axe. Beside, her whole life was in her children, for her marriage was the not uncommon one of a lovely young girl, ignorant of herself, and of her capacities for feeling, to a man of suitable age and position because he chose her. He was an honorable, kind-hearted, well-educated (as it is called) and of good sense, but a mere man of business who had never dreamed of what such a woman as she needs in domestic life. He kept her in a good house, with a good wardrobe, was even in his temper, and indulgent to her wishes, but he did not know what it was to be companionable, the friend, much less the lover, and if he had he would not have had time, for his was the swift crowded course of an American business life. So she pined and grew dull, she knew not why, something was wanting she could not tell what, but there was a dreariness, a blank, she tormented herself that she was so ungrateful to a kind Providence, which had given her so much for want of which the many suffer; she tried to employ herself for the poor, she gave her heart to her children. Still she languished and the first blow found so little life to resist it, that she fell a speedy victim.

Perhaps it was well so, and yet I know not. Beside my own feeling of infinite loss there has been a bitter sense that had

she lived there was enough in me corresponding with her
unconscious wants to have aroused her intellect and occupied
her affections.... 'Twere too bitter to feel that all her lovely
young life was wasted in the sand, but that all around I see
such mutilation of lives, that I must transfer my hope for the
rest to future spheres.... *Margaret Fuller, c. 1840*

*My mother was thirty-seven years old when I was born. When
I was big enough to know her well, she was already an aging
woman who had passed the summit of renown. And yet it is
the celebrated scientist who is strangest to me—probably
because the idea that she was a "celebrated scientist" did not
occupy the mind of Marie Curie. It seems to me, rather, that I
have always lived near the poor student, haunted by dreams,
who was Marya Sklodovska long before I came into the world.*

*And to this young girl Marie Curie still bore a resemblance
on the day of her death. A hard and long and dazzling career
had not succeeded in making her greater or less, in sanctifying
or debasing her. She was on that last day just as gentle,
stubborn, timid and curious about all things as in the days of
her obscure beginnings....*

The creature who wanted us to be invulnerable was herself
too tender, too delicate, too much gifted for suffering. She,
who had voluntarily accustomed us to be undemonstrative,
would no doubt have wished, without confessing it, to have
us embrace and cajole her more. She, who wanted us to be
insensitive, shriveled with grief at the least sign of indifference.
Never did she put our "insensibility" to the test by chastizing
us for our pranks. The traditional punishments, from a harmless
box on the ear to "standing in the corner" or being deprived

of pudding, were unknown at home. Unknown, too, were cries and scenes: my mother would not allow anybody to raise his voice, whether in anger or in joy. One day when Irène had been impertinent, she wanted to "make an example" and decided not to speak to her for two days. These hours were a painful trial for her and for Irène—but, of the two of them, the more punished was Marie: unsettled, wandering miserably about the mournful house, she suffered more than her daughter.

Like a great many children, we were probably selfish and inattentive to shades of feeling. Just the same we perceived the charm, the restrained tenderness and the hidden grace of her we called—in the first line of our letters spotted with ink, stupid little letters which, tied up with confectioners' ribbons, Marie kept until her death—"Darling Mé," "My sweet darling," "My sweet," or else, most often, "Sweet Mé."

Sweet, too sweet "Mé," who could hardly be heard, who spoke to us almost timidly, who wanted to be neither feared nor respected nor admired . . . . Sweet Mé who, along the years, neglected completely to apprise us that she was not a mother like every other mother, not a professor crushed under daily tasks, but an exceptional human being, an illustrious woman.

Eve Curie

Mama played what she called a French harp, and whose proper name is, I believe, a harmonica . . . . When Mama played the French harp, the playing wasn't just an exercise of breath and lips but of her whole body, which at that time was buggy-whip slim and supple. There was no foot stomping or shoulder rocking. But she had a body, and she had a movement. Oh, yes. Perhaps it was more like a pulse. The movement took place, as I remember it, at about an inch above the straight-backed chair on which she sat when she played. She was all spirit at those times and weightless, nothing but music and a tendency to take off . . . .

When Mama played the French harp, I got into a corner where my tears couldn't be seen. I sat on the floor . . . . The coal-oil lamp on the stand table in the middle of the room didn't reach far enough into corners to light up tears.

Mama played all kinds of songs, but most were of the South and the Civil War . . . . There were soldiers still tenting on the campgrounds, we were far from the old folks at home, and Massa was in the cold, cold ground. When Mama played "My Darling Nellie Gray," darling Nellie had truly been taken away, and no one would ever see darling Nellie again. The whole sorrow of that girl and of slavery and of human suffering was in that song when Mama played it.

She played other songs, too. Hymns. Sousa's marches. She liked whatever had feeling in it and was spirited.

She played one spirited song whose words were as strange as any I have ever heard. It was called "Few Days," and its chorus ran, "I am glad that I was born to die. Few days, few days. From grief and woe my soul shall fly, I'm on my journey home."

She sang that song ironically on days when everything went wrong: the days when the Santa Anas blew, the clothesline collapsed, the washday beans burned, on days when Myron fell into a clump of cactus, and Old Silver, defeated in battle, crawled under the house and howled for hours; when ground squirrels proved, unlike the tree squirrels of Southern Indiana, inedible in a stew. Then she sang, "Few days, few days. From grief and woe my soul shall fly, I'm on my journey home. Our camp is in the wilderness, our camp is in the wilderness, but we are going home."

The songbook said that this song was to be played *con spirito,* and thus Mama played it; as, in fact, she played every song. The day might be sad, the heart filled with tears, but the song was *con spirito*. Always. "Ships That Pass in the Night." "The Jealous Lover." "The Kidnapped Child." "The Old Rugged Cross." *Con spirito, con spirito*.   *Jessamyn West*

In winter my mother goes away,
looking for missing dead, stones, ghosts that never stir the
  air
The barking of dogs follows her into the vapor of sunrise.

I am learning the distances.
The stars are hard to see, she walks through crowds of
  people,
falling sand, rooms full of cold.

Birds rise over her shoulders,
a streak of blood.
On the horizon she lifts her hand to warn me.
                                        Del Marie Rogers

MY MOTHER, WHO CAME FROM CHINA,
WHERE SHE NEVER SAW SNOW

In the huge, rectangular room, the ceiling
a machinery of pipes and fluorescent lights,
ten rows of women hunch over machines,
their knees pressing against pedals
and hands pushing the shiny fabric thick as tongues
through metal and thread.
My mother bends her head to one of these machines.
Her hair is coarse and wiry, black as burnt scrub.
She wears glasses to shield her intense eyes.
A cone of orange thread spins. Around her,
talk flutters harshly in Toisan wah.
Chemical stings. She pushes cloth
through a pounding needle, under, around, and out,
breaks thread with a snap against fingerbone, tooth.
Sleeve after sleeve, sleeve.
It is easy. The same piece.
For eight or nine hours, sixteen bundles maybe,
250 sleeves to ski coats, all the same.
It is easy, only once she's run the needle
through her hand. She earns money
by each piece, on a good day,
thirty dollars. Twenty-four years.
It is frightening how fast she works.
She and the women who were taught sewing
terms in English as Second Language.
Dull thunder passes through their fingers.

Laureen Mar

151

Each evening I watch my mother fight
the meaning of words without pictures.

She groups them like birds in a tree.
When she speaks, they career in the wind.

She believes I dreamed. I dream. I will dream.
But does not understand the verb "could."

She thinks we were taught to say "I's" in school,
where to place our tongue, how to move our lips.

Her words do not end with consonants.
They tilt upwards, cling to the air like leaves.

Laureen Mar

"Git' out of my house or I'll throw you out!"

My mother had her arms about Helen. "If she goes out in this night, John, I go with her."

"Yer're a nice wife to talk of goin' out in the streets with a woman like that! You let her go an' come here!"

My mother stood, straight and slender, her face ashen-colored like the face of a wounded coal miner I had seen long ago, a few minutes before he died. Her blue-black eyes glistened... where had I seen such horrible eyes before.... I remembered... why... long ago... I must have been no more than four... I killed a kitten... clodded it to death in the road because it was strange and I pretended it was dangerous.... its eyes in its death agony looked like those of my mother, now.

"Come here!!" my father bellowed at my mother.

But she stood with her arms about Helen.

152

"You come here or I'll break all the furniture in this God damned house!"

My mother continued standing in icy silence, her eyes glistening. With a grunt my father flung out of the back door.

After my mother had defied him about Helen and showed with each passing day that she no longer cared for life, he had become more and more violent. At night I heard hard, bitter weeping, but the door leading into their bedroom was locked. The horror of uncertainty hung over everything.

That year women were given the vote in our State. My mother's chin raised itself just a bit but she held her peace. She was not a talking woman.

"Howrye goin' to vote?" my father asked her.

She did not reply. Quarrels followed . . . he did the quarreling. At last a weapon had been put into her hands. At least she felt it so. He threatened her, but still she would not answer. On election day he threatened to leave home if she didn't tell him. But, without answering, she walked out of the house as if he did not exist. That night he asked a question that was a command:

"D'ye mean to tell me how you voted or not?"

"I don't mean to!"

The next morning she stood on the kitchen porch and he sat on his wagon outside, holding the reins, ready to drive away. My heart was heavy and I felt sick. He asked one more question, but she just stood quietly with her hands folded, and did not answer. Then he went. My mother's frail body braced itself anew.

Agnes Smedley

when mama came here as a gold panner,
she climbed the Chilkoot pass
her long skirts trailin
through snow three feet high
and ice makin her snowblind,
fifty pound rucksack
baby under one arm
when mama came here as a gold panner,
said she was spread so thin
she felt like glass

spread so thin there was holes
in her pie dough, wildberry cobbler
she made'n sold to miners, while
by hand she washed their clothes
with lye soap she'd made by hand,
didn't work fast enough, the men
they'd slap her down back then
was what they did with women
was what they did with cows,
when mama came here as a gold panner,
she felt like glass

like winter ice with the rations
eaten when Mama's hair turned
white as mine, I know
cause she cut'n knotted it into flowers
after doin miner's mendin,
pressed em in her Bible kept
between her sewing basket and darning egg
when mama came here as a gold panner,
said she was spread so thin
she felt like glass...

spread so thin there was holes
in her pie dough, frayed
like the miner's socks she mended,
like her broken kitchen window
spider cracks runnin to the sill
to the water-soaked and rotten window sash,
the hole where the hunter's bullet
winged the pane spider veined
like her upper thighs
when mama came here as a gold panner,
said she was spread so thin

spread so thin she felt like glass
Jana Harris

I am my mother's daughter,
a small woman of large longings.

Energy hurled through her
confined and fierce as in a wind
tunnel. Born to a mean
harried poverty crosshatched
by spidery fears and fitfully
lit by the explosions
of politics, she married her way
at length into the solid workingclass:
a box of house, a car she could
not drive, a TV set kept turned
to the blare of football,
terrifying power tools, used wall
to wall carpeting protected
by scatter rugs.

Out of backyard posies
permitted to fringe
the proud hanky lawn
her imagination hummed
and made honey,
occasionally exploding
in mad queen swarms.

I am her only novel.

Marge Piercy

She lived in a 4-room house on a working class street for 20 years. Over the years she spoke less and less. She drew in; lost year by year the habit of speaking. She smiled. She nodded. I could make her laugh, or blush. Sometimes she held me, rocked me. But she had no words to give. What she wanted to say became too big to be sayable, and the habit of not speaking too fixed. Or, as she said, much later: Too big to put your tongue around.

Some days the restraints broke, and words came. Words about cars that drove by in the night, but she knew who they were. Words about voices that came over the radio, but she was not fooled, she knew who they were. Words about turning pictures to the wall: It wasn't safe to look at them.

She never asked why do I ride in the back of the car with the children while another woman rides up front with my husband? She never asked why is a mother never a wife never a lover? She never asked why does my husband call me Bertha when my name is Alice?

They put her away in a place for people who can't speak, or speak in tongues. After many years she stopped being angry. Then she was calm, distracted, utterly amiable. But her foot moved constantly, involuntarily. And she had gained the ability to speak, but lost a life to speak of.   *May Stevens*

For many years I . . . never imagined my mother any way other than the person she had become before I was born. She was just a fact of life when I was growing up; someone to be worried about and cared for; an invalid who lay in bed with eyes closed and lips moving in occasional response to voices only she could hear; a woman to whom I brought an endless stream of toast and coffee, bologna sandwiches and dime pies, in a child's version of what meals should be. She was a loving, intelligent, terrorized woman who tried hard to clean our littered house whenever she emerged from her private world, but who could rarely be counted on to finish one task. In many ways, our roles were reversed: I was the mother and she was the child. Yet that didn't help her, for she still worried about me with all the intensity of a frightened mother, plus the special fears of her own world full of threats and hostile voices.

Even then I supposed I must have known that, years before she was thirty–five and I was born, she had been a spirited, adventurous young woman who struggled out of a working-class family and into college, who found work she loved and continued to do, even after she was married and my older sister was there to be cared for . . . .

She had suffered her first "nervous breakdown," as she and everyone else called it, before I was born and when my sister was about five. It followed years of trying to take care of a baby, be the wife of a kind but financially irresponsible man with show-business dreams, and still keep her much-loved job as reporter and newspaper editor. After many months in a sanitorium, she was pronounced recovered. That is, she was able to take care of my sister again, to move away from the city and the job she loved, and to work with my father at the isolated rural lake in Michigan he was trying to transform into a resort worthy of the big dance bands of the 1930s.

But she was never again completely without the spells of depression, anxiety, and visions into some other world that eventually were to turn her into the nonperson I remember . . . .

It was a strange experience to look into those brown eyes I had seen so often and realize suddenly how much they were like my own. For the first time, I realized that she might really be my mother.

I began to think about the many pressures that might have led up to that first nervous breakdown: leaving my sister whom she loved very much with a grandmother whose values my mother didn't share; trying to hold on to a job she loved but was being asked to leave by her husband; wanting very much to go with a woman friend to pursue their own dreams in New York; falling in love with a coworker at the newspaper who frightened her by being more sexually attractive, more supportive of her work than my father, and perhaps the man she should have married; and finally nearly bleeding to death with a miscarriage because her own mother had little faith in doctors and refused to get help . . . .

At the hospital and later when Ruth told me stories of her past, I used to say, "But why didn't you leave? Why didn't you take the job? Why didn't you marry the other man?" She would always insist it didn't matter, she was lucky to have my sister and me. If I pressed hard enough, she would add, "If I'd left you never would have been born."

I always thought but never had the courage to say: *But you might have been born instead.* . . .

I can only guess what she might have become. . . .

It was she who introduced me to books and a respect for them, to poetry that she knew by heart, and to the idea that

159

you could never criticize someone unless you "walked miles in their shoes."

It was she who sold that Toledo house, the only home she had, with the determination that the money be used to start me in college. She gave both her daughters the encouragement to leave home for four years of independence that she herself had never had....

I miss her, but perhaps no more in death than I did in life.

Gloria Steinem

Certainly there she was, in the very centre of that great Cathedral space which was childhood; there she was from the very first. My first memory is of her lap; the scratch of some beads on her dress comes back to me as I pressed my cheek against it. Then I see her in her white dressing gown on the balcony; and the passion flower with the purple star on its petals. Her voice is still faintly in my ears—decided, quick; and in particular the little drops with which her laugh ended—three diminishing ahs... "Ah—ah—ah..." I sometimes end a laugh that way myself....

I hear the tinkle of her bracelets, made of twisted silver, given her by Mr. Lowell, as she went about the house; especially as she came up at night to see if we were asleep, holding a candle shaded; this is a distinct memory, for, like all children, I lay awake sometimes and longed for her to come. Then she told me to think of all the lovely things I could imagine. Rainbows and bells....

By the time we, her children, knew her, she was the most prompt, practical and vivid of human beings. It was as though she had made up her mind definitely upon certain great matters and was never after troubled to consider herself at all; but every deed and word had the bright, inexorable, swift stamp of something struck clearly by a mass of hoarded experience. Four children were born to her; there were four others already, older, demanding other care; she taught us, was their companion, and soothed, cheered, inspired, nursed, deceived your grandfather; and any one coming for help found her invincibly upright in her place, with time to give, earnest consideration, and the most practical sympathy. Her relations with people indeed were all through her life remarkable; and after her second marriage ... [she spent] herself more freely than ever in the service of others ....

Her view of the world had come to be very comprehensive; she seemed to watch, like some wise Fate, the birth, growth, flower and death of innumerable lives all round her, with a constant sense of the mystery that encircled them, not now so sceptical as of old, and [with] a perfectly definite idea of the help that was possible and of use. Her intellectual gifts had always been those that find their closest expression in action; she had great clearness of insight, sound judgement, humour, and a power of grasping very quickly the real nature of someone's circumstances, and so arranging that the matter, whatever it was, fell into its true proportions at once. Sometimes with her natural impetuosity, she took it on herself to despatch difficulties with a high hand, like some commanding Empress. But most often I think her service, when it was not purely practical, lay in simply helping people by the light of her judgement and experience, to see what they really meant or felt .... All her gifts had something swift, decisive, witty even, in their nature; so that there could be no question of dulness or drudgery in her daily work, however lugubrious it seemed of itself .... While she was there the whole of that interminable

161

and incongruous procession which is the life of a large family, went merrily; with exquisite humour in its incidents very often, or something grotesque or impressive in its arrangement, perpetually lit up by her keen attention, her amazing sense of the life that is in the weakest or most threadbare situations . . . .

In addition to all her other labours she took it on herself to teach us our lessons, and thus established a very close and rather trying relationship, for she was of a quick temper, and least of all inclined to spare her children. . . . But in no other way could we have learnt, in the short time we had, so much of her true nature, obscured by none of those graceful figments which interpose themselves generally in the gulf which lies between a middle-aged woman and her children. It might have been better, as it certainly would have tired her less, had she allowed that some of those duties could be discharged for her. But she was impetuous, and also a little imperious; so conscious of her own burning will that she could scarcely believe that there was not something quicker and more effective in her action than in another's. Thus when your grandfather was ill she would never suffer a nurse to be with him, nor could she believe that a governess would teach us as well as she did. And apart from economy, which always weighed with her, she had come to attach a desperate importance to the saving of time, as though she saw heap themselves all round her, duties and desires, and time to embrace them slipped from her and left her with grasping fingers. She had constantly in mind that comprehensive view of the final proportions of things which I have noticed; for her words were never trivial. . . .

There it always was, the common life of the family, very merry, very stirring, crowded with people; and she was the centre; it was herself. This was proved on May 5th 1895. For after that day there was nothing left of it.   *Virginia Woolf*

1

2

3

4

5

6

7

8

9

10

11

12

13

14

15

16

17

18

19

20

21

22

23

24

25

26

27

28

29

30

31

AUGUST
Other Carers, Tenders: Grandmothers, Mammies, Sisters, Teachers

Out of her own body she pushed
silver thread, light, air
Paula Gunn Allen

That from which these things are born
That by which they live
That to which they return at death
Try to know that
Carolyn Forche

Grandma was a kind of first-aid station.
Lillian Smith

GRANDMOTHER

Out of her own body she pushed
silver thread, light, air
and carried it carefully on the dark, flying
where nothing moved.

Out of her body she extruded
shining wire, life, and wove the light
on the void.

From beyond time,
beyond oak* trees and bright clear water flow,
she was given the work of weaving the strands
of her body, her pain, her vision
into creation, and the gift of having created,
to disappear.

After her,
the women and the men weave blankets into tales of life,
memories of light and ladders,
infinity-eyes, and rain.
After her I sit on my laddered rain-bearing rug
and mend the tear with string.

Paula Gunn Allen

* I am a member of Oak Clan.

That from which these things are born
That by which they live
That to which they return at death
Try to know that . . .

Anna's hands were like wheat rolls
Shelling snow peas, Anna's hands
Are both dead, they were Uzbek,
Uzbek hands known for weaving fine rugs

Eat Bread and Salt and Speak the Truth

She was asking me to go with her
To the confrontation of something
That was sacred and eternal
It was a timeless, timeless thing
Nothing of her old age or my childhood
Came between us . . .

Mother of God
I tell you this
Dushenka
You work your life
You have nothing . . .

She had drawn apple skin
Tightly bent feet
Pulled babushkas and rosary beads
On which she paid for all of us

She knew how much grease
How deep to seed
That cukes were crawlers

Every morning at five she would market
Or wake me to pick and hoe, crows
Cackling between us, Slovakia swear words
Whenever I stopped to feed them ...

Heavy sweatered winter woman
Buried the October before I was grown
She would take gladiolas to the priest
Like sword spouts they fumed near her bed

After raising my father and nine others
In a foreign country
Find yourself a good man
Get married
There is nothing left ...

She could hear snow touch chopped wood
Her room smelled of advent candles
Cake flour clung to her face ...

I want to ask you why I live
And we go back apart across the field
Why I am here and will have to feel the way I die

It was all over my face
Grandma flipped kolačy rolls
Dunked her hands in bowls of water
Looked at me
Wrung rags into the stoop
Kept it from me
Whatever she saw

Carolyn Forche

AUGUST

I can imagine the pain and the strength of my great great grandmothers who were slaves and my great great grandmothers who were Cherokee Indians trapped on reservations. I remembered my great grandmother who walked everywhere rather than sit in the back of the bus. I think about North Carolina and my home town and I remember the women of my grandmother's generation: strong, fierce women who could stop you with a look out of the corners of their eyes. Women who walked with majesty; who could wring a chicken's neck and scale a fish. Who could pick cotton, plant a garden, and sew without a pattern. Women who boiled clothes white in big black cauldrons and who hummed work songs and lullabys. Women who visited the elderly, made soup for the sick and shortnin bread for the babies.

Women who delivered babies, searched for healing roots and brewed medicines. Women who darned sox and chopped wood and layed bricks. Women who could swim rivers and shoot the head off a snake. Women who took passionate responsibility for their children and for their neighbors' children too. *Assata Shakur*

When the Civil War ended, the homeplace broke into fragments .... So Little Grandma, the ninety pounds of her there were, took over. She taught her nine boys how to plow, she plowed too, to show them; they planted the fields together, they hoed and tended; and their mother was always there helping, making it seem like fun, while the two small daughters played dolls near by and the baby lay asleep under a tree near the branch.

One day, as it slept in the shade on the cool bank of the branch, Little Grandma heard a snapping of twigs and saw, coming down the edge of the water, a swamp cat. A "painter." He was almost as close as she; not quite, but he could spring swiftly and she knew it. She did not take her eyes off him as she started slowly toward the baby ....

I have heard it all of my life, this story. Little Grandma ....would sit by her hearth, wrapped up in her crocheted shawl, stirring her fire now and then, and tell us. And while she told it, we would be roasting pecans in the ashes, or sweet potatoes—because we knew that potatoes had been cooked that way, when she was young, and we wanted to try things the way she had done them. She would tell it and always it was a legend of reassurance, a story of human strength able to deal with what comes to a person day by day. Things are like that, she made us feel—this little lady who was more than eighty years old and still so slight and so strong. The swamp panther is always killed before it reaches the baby ....

Then she'd say in exactly the same tone, Better look to your nuts, and we'd scrabble for them in the ashes and draw them out and cool them and they were brown-smelling and fragrant to eat. Or we'd turn over the roasting potatoes and she would tell us other stories about those days when dangers seemed to be outside cf people and never inside their own minds.

And always there was in her room—this room which we called "Little Grandma's" for years after she was gone—a feeling that nothing could win over life, not even death. Nothing could get into the room with her unless it shrank down littler than Little Grandma....

Grandma was a kind of first-aid station, or a Red Cross nurse, who took up where the battle ended, accepting us and our little sobbing sins, gathering the whole of us into her lap, restoring us to health and confidence by her amazing faith in life and in a mortal's strength to meet it.... Moments when we shrank in sudden fear from life, even from ourselves, Little Grandma called us into her room, drew us close around her hearth, and somehow healed our bruises.   *Lillian Smith*

I have an entire notebook, seventy-five pages, both sides of each page filled with Mama's continuing account of the work of a woman's day in the 1890s. Soap making, cider making, apple-butter making. Drying of apples, corn, peaches. Knitting stockings, crocheting edging for pillow shams, shimmies, nightdresses, drawers. Gathering fox grapes, hickory nuts, butternuts, beechnuts. Making sorghum, maple syrup, yeast, twisted paper lamplighters. Pickling peaches, pears, cucumbers, corn. "Putting down" comb honey, lard, fried sausage, sauerkraut. They braided rags for rugs, then sewed the braids together. They cut rags into strips, which were then woven into "rag carpets." They raised the geese and plucked them for feather beds. They pieced the quilts in patterns fanciful, strange, and sweet; put them on frames and quilted them with tiny decorative stitches; they made and tied the comforters. They put together and embroidered the mosaic of the many-colored crazy quilts.

They did all this and more. Mary Frances [my grandmother] did all this, "with her arms and body," with her little hands (her wedding ring goes just to the first joint of my little finger). She did it all without the joy in her husband that lightens a woman's work . . . .

[Grandma McManaman's] head-start school was not discontinued when we left for California. Books and magazines arrived; poems clipped from papers or copied by hand were received, with instructions to memorize and recite. I don't know how this was managed. Did I go to my teacher and say, "I have memorized a poem my grandma sent me, and she wants me to recite it"? However it was accomplished, I recited them. They were, for the most part, "Let us now be up and doing" poems. "My head is bloody but unbowed" poems. "If you can keep your head when all about you" poems. Poems of strife and resistance, and finally, if nothing could be done, "When God sorts out the weather and sends rain, why, rain's my choice." I was a kind of Western outpost in that battle, perhaps against her very nature, that Grandma was waging. She sent me dresses—natural linen embroidered in red; lavender so-isette smocked with white silk—to wear when I recited. She always wanted to know how I did. Did I forget? Did I speak up? Did I stand straight? When the reports were good, she must have felt that the center still held, though at the edges there were signs of fraying.

She died saying, "Hurry, hurry, hurry," not to a nurse, not to anyone at her bedside, but to herself—little Doll McManaman, who had accomplished so much less than she had planned.   *Jessamyn West*

177

My grandmother wanted then a report on our household routine. Had we got the washing done, had we got the washing dried, had we got the ironing done? The baking? My father's socks mended? She wished to be of help. She would make biscuits and muffins, a pie (did we have a pie?); bring the mending and she would do it. The ironing too. She would go out to our place for a day, to help, as soon as the roads were clear. I was too embarrassed to think we needed help, and I especially tried to ward off the visits. Before my grandmother came I would be obliged to try to clean the house, reorganize the cupboards as much as possible, shove certain disgraces— a roasting-pan I had never got round to scrubbing, a basket of torn clothes I had told her were already mended—under the sink or the beds. But I never cleaned thoroughly enough, my reorganization proved to be haphazard, the disgraces came unfailingly to light, and it was clear how we failed, how disastrously we fell short of that ideal of order and cleanliness, household decency, which I as much as anybody else believed in. Believing in it was not enough. And it was not just for myself but for my mother that I had to feel shame.

"Your mother isn't well, she cannot get around to things," said my grandmother, in a voice that indicated doubt as to how much would have been gotten around to, in any case.

"She isn't going [home]," my grandmother said, still lightly. "She isn't walking out into that storm."

"It isn't a *storm*," I said, looking for help towards the window, which showed solid white.

My grandmother put her cup down, rattling it on the saucer. "All right. Go then. Just go. Go if you want to. Go and get frozen to death."

I had never heard my grandmother lose control before. I

had never imagined she could. It seems strange to me now, but the fact is that I had never heard anything like plain hurt or anger in her voice, or seen it on her face. Everything had been indirect, calmly expressed. Her judgments had seemed remote, full of traditional authority, not personal. The abdication here was what amazed me. There were tears in her voice, and when I looked at her there were tears in her eyes and then pouring down her face. She was weeping, she was furious and weeping.

"Never mind then. You just go. Go and get yourself frozen to death like what happened to poor Susie Heferman."

I ate a large supper. No more mention was made of Susie Heferman.

I understand various things now, though my understanding them is not of much use to anybody . . . . My grandmother had schooled herself, watched herself, learned what to do and say; she had understood the importance of acceptance, had yearned for it, had achieved it, had known there was a possibility of not achieving it. Aunt Madge had never known that. My grandmother could feel endangered by my mother, could perhaps even understand—at some level she would always have to deny—those efforts of my mother's that she so successfully, and never quite openly, ridiculed and blamed.

I understand that my grandmother wept angrily for Susie Heferman and also for herself, that she knew how I longed for home, and why. She knew and did not understand how this had happened or how it could have been different or how she herself, once so baffled and struggling, had become another old woman whom people deceived and placated and were anxious to get away from.   *Alice Munro*

179

AUGUST

MARY GRAVELY JONES

We had no petnames, no diminutives for you,
always the formal guest under my father's roof:
you were "Grandmother Jones" and you visited rarely.
I see you walking up and down the garden,
restless, southern-accented, reserved, you did not seem
my mother's mother or anyone's grandmother.
You were Mary, widow of William, and no matriarch,
yet smoldering to the end with frustrate life,
ideas nobody listened to, least of all my father.
One summer night you sat with my sister and me
in the wooden glider long after twilight,
holding us there with streams of pent-up words.
You could quote every poet I had ever heard of,
had read *The Opium Eater*, Amiel and Bernard Shaw,
your green eyes looked clenched against opposition.
You married straight out of the convent school,
your background was country, you left an unperformed
typescript of a play about Burr and Hamilton,
you were impotent and brilliant, no one cared
about your mind, you might have ended
elsewhere than in that glider
reciting your unwritten novels to the children.

Adrienne Rich

When I look back now, through that fast-vanishing perspective, it seems to me, though I had suffered every illness known to the childhood of that day, that the happiest years were those between the ages of three and seven, when I lived, with my Mammy Lizzie, a life of wandering adventures. For we sought adventures, not only in the tales we spun at night, while I undressed before the fire, but even in the daytime, when we roamed, hand-in-hand, in search of the fresh and the strange, through the streets and back alleys, and up and down the hills of old Richmond.

My beloved mammy, Lizzie Jones, was an extraordinary character, endowed with an unusual intelligence, a high temper, and a sprightly sense of humor. If fate had yielded her even the slightest advantages of education and opportunity, she might have made a place for herself in the world. But she could neither read nor write . . . . She had an inventive mind, and we were never at a loss for new games or stirring adventures . . . . [Her leaving] was the first real sorrow of my life. It was the beginning of that sense of loss, of exile in solitude, which I was to bear with me to the end.

"As soon as I learn my letters, Mammy, I'm going to teach you yours," I promised. But I never taught her, and to this day, I regret that I did not.   *Ellen Glasgow*

181

My black mother was "mine" only for four years, during which she fed me, dressed me, played with me, watched over me, sang to me, cared for me tenderly and intimately. "Childless" herself, she *was* a mother. She was slim, dignified, and very handsome, and from her I learned—nonverbally—a great deal about the possibilities of dignity in a degrading situation.... Twenty years later, when I left my parents' house, expecting never to return, my black mother told me: "Yes, I understand how you have to leave and do what you think is right. I once had to break somebody's heart to go and live my life." She died a few years later; I did not see her again.

Adrienne Rich

Sophronia was the first and most certain love of my life. (Years later, when I was a dangerously rebellious young girl, my father would say that if he had been able to afford Sophronia through the years, I would have been under the only control I ever recognized.) She was a tall, handsome, light tan woman— I still have many pictures of the brooding face—who was for me, as for so many other white Southern children, the one and certain anchor so needed for the young years, so forgotten after that. (It wasn't that way for us: we wrote and met as often as possible until she died when I was in my twenties, and the first salary check I ever earned she returned to me in the form of a gold chain.)

Lillian Hellman

I knew that my old nurse who had cared for me through long months of illness, who had given me refuge when a little sister took my place as the baby of the family, who soothed me, fed me, delighted me with her stories and games, let me fall asleep on her warm, deep breast, was not [supposed to be] worthy of the passionate love I felt for her but must be given instead a half-smiled-at affection . . . I knew but I never believed it that the deep respect I felt for her, the tenderness, the love, was a childish thing which every normal child outgrows . . . and that somehow—though it seemed impossible to my agonized heart—I too must outgrow these feelings . . . . I learned to cheapen with tears and sentimental talk of "my old mammy" one of the profound relationships of my life. *Lillian Smith*

TEACHER

I make my children promises in wintery afternoons
like lunchtime stories
when my feet hurt from talking too much
and not enough movement except in my own
worn down at the heel shoes
except in the little circle of broken down light
I am trapped in
the intensities of my own (our) situation
where what we need and do not have
deadens us
and promises sound like destruction
white snowflakes clog the passages
drifting through the halls and corridors
while I tell stories with no ending
at lunchtime
the children's faces bear uneasy smiles
like a heavy question
I provide food with a frightening efficiency
the talk is free/dom meaning state
condition of being
We are elementary forces colliding in free fall

Audre Lorde

One of the things about the Notre Dame nuns who educated me was their sense that all of us were great women of Notre Dame . . . . You were supposed to accomplish something, you were supposed to work in your community, you were supposed to be of service. And there they were, leading their lives in that way, university professors . . . . One of my teachers, Sister Catherine Anne, at the end of the ninth grade, wrote on a paper: "Keep working diligently, Mary Helen, and one day you will *do* things." I cut out that little comment she made on my English paper and I saved it and I sent it to her after *Black Eyed Susans* was published in 1975. I had saved it from 1955 to 1975. I never threw it away. Because that is what those nuns did, they said Get Out and Do Something.

When I started teaching high school, I taught for two years and another of my nun teachers, Sister Luke, called me up and said, "Now that's enough, it's time to go to graduate school." She sat down and wrote all the recommendations, and at the end of the year I had five scholarships to graduate school, so I went on . . . .

Mary Helen Washington

AUGUST

RUISE

I never thought to see us
grow old, our waists thicken, our
children move so quickly toward being women and men.
I have of course; but to see
the woman of your hands
is not to know the girl
who took the womanme in
saw so clearly what it was
that would save me for my
self and so let me be a
child again.
        The long waisted
body   the long straight neck will
soon disappear in folds of
aging flesh but not age not
added flesh not even death
could wipe away what the strength
of your love and anger trace
in the still deepening earth
tones of your face.
            I have no
daughters to be the woman
you are and your own is still
becoming.

     aerated loam
and fire   the song some bird will
sing   sum and homage   sista
* sista   sista   been and is*

       Sherley Anne Williams
      186

For a mother-in-law

The place to begin is not your death,
nor my divorce. It is not at the priest-
less wedding of your Catholic son
to a Protestant. Perhaps the best place
to begin is in the kitchen where
you stand before me now in memory.

You teach me to dice vegetables
all so uniform no one would guess
they've come from things as varied
as carrots and potatoes. Romaine
lettuce leaves are delicate as baby
skin and must be laid to dry
on white linen tea towels.

Half a glass of red wine in your hand,
you saute the vegetables, giggling
over some silliness between us.
When you laugh so hard that tears
come and you remove thick-lensed
glasses to wipe your eyes, still laughing,
I see the young woman you must have been,
striking out for a California modeling
career in defiance of your mother.

My guess is that since the first day
of your first-born you've been waiting
for the slap your mother smarted with
the day you left, for, as we cook,
the things that you refuse to know
about your own children are everywhere
but in our talk: my being on The Pill;

187

Cathy's living in sin with her boyfriend;
David's fighting with his wife.

While the sauce thickens, you show me
the landscape you're working on.
Like your make-up and your hair,
your paintings are faithful to magazine
photographs. Grasping hairbrush
or paintbrush, your hands are the devotion
of a manuscript illuminator painting again
and again someone else's vision.

Beside each dinner plate you place
a cup of vitamins especially selected
for each person. You are always
on the watch for pale complexions,
dark-ringed eyes and listlessness
you have faith vitamins will cure.

Yesterday your son told me
that in the last five years
the fears you never allowed
yourself had one by one come
home to you: your oldest
daughter, Laura, dead—your happy
child, the one who watched
for hours as you put just the right
light in the sky; other divorces;
your husband's desertion;
your youngest daughter, Mary,
pregnant at fifteen.

I want to believe
that the children who had trailed

away from all you were
faded in your last months
as you watched this daughter's
belly rise, that you could almost
ignore what grew in your own breast,
that you could almost feel
the child's head resting there,
solid, absolute.

Judith Sornberger

1

2

3

4

5

6

7

8

9

10

11

12

13

14

15

16

17

18

19

20

21

22

23

24

25

26

27

28

29

30

31

SEPTEMBER
The Afterview and At The Last

"What do you do with mother love and mother wit when the babies are grown and gone away?"

Joanne Greenberg

The responsibility of Pathos is almost more than the responsibility of Care.

Emily Dickinson

Her mouth was slightly open, but her breathing took up so much of her strength that she could not talk. But she looked at me, or so I felt, to speak for her. She depended on me for a voice.

Zora Neale Hurston

Last night I dreamed once more that I had a baby. There was much in the dream that was painful, but I recall one sensation distinctly. I was holding the tiny infant in my arms and I had a feeling of great bliss as I thought that I could go on always holding it in my arms. It would be one year old and then only two, and I would not have to give it away.

Kaethe Kollwitz, at age 49

"But—isn't it a shock, usually a fatal shock, to transplant an old, deep-rooted tree? And was I not deep-rooted in usefulness and now wrenched away from it, all those living fibers that brought life to me torn loose, withering and drying up? Can the few small roots that have not been cut—those dry little Reading Club and Improvement Society roots—can they keep *me* alive who drew life abundant from a thousand others? And is not dying painful? Those roots that are left to me, they should be stronger, do you say? I should have given more of myself to them when I was younger, should I? But, see here— I don't complain of this, or glory in it, I state the fact—if I had not given all of myself to learn the art I had to practice, I would have failed. All of myself was not too much to learn how to give my children what they needed. Everybody knows that he who practices an art must give it all he has, or fail.

"Suppose you said to a painter of sixty—my age—who had given all his life to his lovely, living, rewarding art, 'Lay down your brushes now. You've finished your pictures. You'll only spoil them if you go on fussing with them. And don't be so unreasonable and self-centered as to feel sad about this. If you still want to do something, can't you learn how to put on wall-paper instead?'"

Dorothy Canfield Fisher

197

Now they put a baby in her lap. Do not ask me, she would have liked to beg. Enough the worn face of Vivi, the remembered grandchildren. I cannot, cannot . . . .

Cannot what? Unnatural grandmother, not able to make herself embrace a baby.

She lay there in the bed of the two little girls, her new hearing aid turned full, listening to the sound of the children going to sleep, the baby's fretful crying and hushing, the clatter of dishes being washed and put away. They thought she slept. Still she rode on.

It was not that she had not loved her babies, her children. The love—the passion of tending—had risen with the need like a torrent; and like a torrent drowned and immolated all else. But when the need was done—oh the power that was lost in the painful damming back and drying up of what still surged, but had nowhere to go. Only the thin pulsing left that could not quiet, suffering over lives one felt, but could no longer hold nor help.

On that torrent she had borne them to their own lives, and the riverbed was desert long years now. Not there would she dwell, a memoried wraith. Surely that was not all, surely there was more. Still the springs, the springs were in her seeking. Somewhere an older power that beat for life. Somewhere coherence, transport, community. If they would but leave her in the air now stilled of clamor, in the reconciled solitude, to journey on.

And they put a baby in her lap. Immediacy to embrace, and the breath of *that* past: warm flesh like this that had claims and nuzzled away all else and with lovely mouths devoured; hot-living like an animal—intensely and now; the turning maze; the long drunkenness; the drowning into needing and being needed. Severely she looked back—and the shudder seized

198

her again, and the sweat. Not that way. Not there, not now could she, not yet . . . .

And all that visit, she could not touch the baby.

Tillie Olsen

She pursued her innocent ends with increasing anxiety. She rose early, then earlier, then earlier still. She wanted to have the world to herself, deserted, in the form of a little enclosure with a trellis and a sloping roof. She wanted the jungle to be virgin but, even so, inhabited only by swallows, cats, and bees, and the huge spider balancing atop his wheel of lace silvered by the night. . . . She got up at six, then at five, and at the end of her life a little red lamp wakened her, in winter, long before the Angelus smote the black air. In those moments while it was still night my mother used to sing, falling silent as soon as anyone was able to hear. The lark also sings while it is mounting toward the palest, least inhabited part of the sky. My mother climbed too, mounting ceaselessly up the ladder of the hours, trying to possess the beginning of the beginning. I know what that particular intoxication is like. But what she sought was a red, horizontal ray, and the pale sulphur that comes before the red ray; she wanted the damp wing that the first bee stretches out like an arm. The summer wind, which springs up at the approach of the sun, gave her its first fruits in scents of acacia and woodsmoke; when a horse pawed the ground and whinnied softly in the neighboring stable, she was the first to hear it. On an autumn morning she was the only one to see herself reflected in the first disk of ephemeral ice in the well bucket, before her nail cracked it.

Colette

September 23, 1919. Dear Mother. She is often sick. Then she is downcast, says her head feels so confused. She does not know what to do or where she belongs. And it is so moving when she gravely and dignifiedly takes my hand and gives me heartfelt thanks because we keep her with us. Then I feel such love for her that I could make any sacrifice for her sake. Mother's hardest time is already behind her, the time when she often realized that she was wandering. Now she is usually cheerful; but it is touching to see her at moments even now when she realizes and then feels so helplessly confused.

December 26, 1919. There are days when Mother sleeps most of the time, murmuring softly in her dreams and daydreaming when she is awake. Always about children. Sometimes full of care and fear that they will not come home. But mostly the scenes she sees are very pleasant. The children sleeping in their room. Then she wants to go to wake them, and comes back wondering: where are they? It is really so sweet to see how the dreams and visions and fantasies of so old a mother always return to her children. So after all they were the strongest emotion in her life.   *Kaethe Kollwitz*

To Mrs. J. G. Holland   *about September 1880*
Dear Sister—

The responsibility of Pathos is almost more than the responsibility of Care. Mother will never walk. She still makes her little Voyages from her Bed to her Chair in a Strong Man's Arms–probably that will be all.

Her poor Patience loses it's way and we lead it back–I was telling her Nieces yesterday, who wrote to ask for her, that to read to her–to fan her–to tell her "Health will come Tomorrow" and make the Counterfeit look real . . .this is so ensuing, that I hardly have said, "Good Morning, Mother" when I hear myself saying "Mother, –Good Night–"

Time is short and full, like an outgrown frock. . . .

Emily (Dickinson)

No use waiting for it to stop
raining in my face like a wet towel,
having to catch a plane,
to pick the apples from her tree
and bring them home. . . .

She used to slice them in quarters,
cut through the core,
open the inside out. Fingers
steady on the knife, expert
at stripping things.

Sometimes she split them sideways
into halves to let a star break
from the center with tight seeds,
because I wanted that,
six petals in the flesh.

Flavor of apples inhaled as flowers,
not even biting them.
Apples at lunch or after school
like soup, a fragrance rising
in the steam, eat and be well.

I bring the peeled fruit to her
where she lies, carve it
in narrow sections, celery white,
place them between her fingers,
Mother, eat. And be well.

Sit where her brown eyes
empty out the light, watching

her mind slip backwards
on the pillow, swallowing
apples, swallowing her life.
                    Shirley Kaufman

Tranquilized, she speaks or does not speak;
Immobilized, she goes to & fro invisibly....

Patient, she lies like a paradigm
Elaborate on her fenced high bed because
Her hip-bone snapped. Her doctor
Indicates his neat repair. I flinch
Before her sacredness.

From between those thighs
(Splashed in those days iridescent
With brighter-than-blood mercurochrome)
I thrust into sight thirsting for air;
(So it must have been; so my children came;
So we commit by embodying it, woman to woman,
Our power: to set life free.
She set me free).

Long closed against me, now her flesh
Is a text I guess to read: Is
She in pain? My own flesh aches dumb
For a mummer's gift of touch
We might use to speak ourselves
Against this last fitful light....

                    Marie Ponsot

203

JENNIE LUBELL IS IN A
NURSING HOME IN PROVINCETOWN

My mother has died, but I visit her weekly
At that Eden near the end of Route Six
Where the angels, dressed in traditional white,
Are largely of Portugese descent and have warm eyes.

The long drive weans me from my life.
It is its own limbo—expectancy coming and going . . .

I closed her apartment.
It was a solitary mourning week of packing,
Picking my way through snowbanks after work . . .
And climbing the dark stairs to her lair,
Where so many years she held all help at bay,
So that I could not sleep for worry in my snug suburban
    bed. . . .

How did she hold on so long, half the blood gone from her
    arteries,
Staggering, dizzy, near-blind, and alone? . . .

Well, she topped ninety there, inner ear, ulcers, and all.
Nearly sixteen years since the drunk drove into her,
Crossing Comm Ave on her way from helping Aunt Sarah,
And smashed her head and pelvis, so that she trotted her
    daily circuit
After she healed, listing to starboard like a drunken
    sailor,
Three miles into the wind. Is that why she lasted so long?

Everyone died before her—they went "so young,"
Leaving her alone in a world of indifferent children
"Who care more for dogs than for people.
Who knows? Maybe God will help."

At The Last

God did, perhaps—arrange things
So she landed in this alien final place
Where nobody knows or remembers her
Or treasures her stories—those three-D spells
That peopled my childhood with fairytale worlds
That were her youth.

They are kind here and make her cozy, though her new
    nightgowns
Keep getting lost in the wash. . . .

The rooms are warm and clean. . . .

Inside, someone has knit bright afghans
To bring a cheerful color to white beds.
Mealtimes are very important; inmates gather before time
Like antelope at a water hole, breaking the desert boredom,
The long cascade to ending.

My mother is quieted. Her guts, she explains, have gone out
    of her.
That is literally true, but she means her courage is gone.
Her voice is small and ladylike; no surge of ready rage
Or dazzle of pointed wit stirs her composure . . .
"They take good care of me. You don't need to worry.
They are good people. Some of them." (A flash of the old Ma?)
Her litany is platitudes to keep me warm.
I watch my mother sleeping, a tiny huddle under the bright
    coverlet. . . .

How many years of daily talking are halted here?
What a silence has entered my life!
Better she were fighting—and alive.

* * * *

205

SEPTEMBER

I drive the long lonely road back to my life.
My suspension settles as I enter thicker traffic, jockey for place.
I understand the worth of what is left to me and drive with
   care.
It is important now to move, to engage, to shout aloud,
To wipe out memories of that still shape
Breathing its life away under a gaudy blanket.
Escaping me, our life together, and memory,
Leaving me alone—we are each alone—
For my own dark journey.

Adeline Naiman

As I grew up . . . what was impenetrable to me was my . . . mother's love for her own mother. Between these two there was no generation gap, no chasm. My mother never wracked her brains explaining why she and her mother couldn't "relate". . . Far from dreading her visits—as so many women I know secretly dread their mothers' visits—my mother looked forward to being under the same roof with her. "Mama is coming to stay with us awhile" was a boast, not the presentiment of a nervous breakdown . . . . And though it was an interminable, dusty voyage, my mother was always eager to go to her mama's house. . . .

When I was four, my grandma died. . . .My mother, after weeping into a handkerchief for most of the ceremony, lost control and sobbed and screamed and collapsed on the ground. I could hardly endure the sight of it. Not until years later did it occur to me that she was not quite twenty-five on the day of the funeral, an orphan. But I knew that her love for the woman lying there had in it something that tore the heart out,

206

something I dreaded and did not wish to understand.

I loved my mother, too, but not that way. That love frightened me. Years later, when I encountered the word "atavistic," I knew immediately what it meant. From mother to daughter for a dozen generations, perhaps a hundred thousand, had come this unspoken counsel, this taciturn resolve to work until your skin turned to leather and your back never stopped aching, to do the labor of ten men, if necessary, and to seek in your progeny your only real sense of accomplishment. For such women, their first and perhaps only allegiance was to their children. They would have died for them, like a grizzly bear in her tracks, in a devotion equally unreasoning. . . .

One August morning when I was thirty-three and a long-gone northerner . . . [my mother] had the first of several seizures—an intimation of mortality, a fast and vicious dress rehearsal for her death throes six months hence. . . .

I left my husband and my job in New York and [came] to stay with her full time. . . . The indecent passion she had felt for her mother at last laid hold of me. I couldn't bear the idea of anyone but me waiting on her, cutting up her food in tiny pieces for her, washing her nightgowns, cleaning her house, taking her a bedpan at 3 A.M. . . .

As her spine dissolved and her speech worsened, and she lost the ability to read and write, and she became almost immobile, I took a certain grim pleasure in making her as comfortable as I could. She was doing what she could for me too. . . .

The hospital where she finally went so that she could have injections of morphine (ironically, she almost always refused them; she said they didn't kill the pain but locked her up inside it) was a homey, almost countrified place where the needs of the dying were understood, and always had been.

The nurses brought me a cot so I could spend the nights, and for almost six months I lived there with her. . . .

She never wanted to talk about what was happening to her—the word "cancer" was not in her vocabulary. I felt, uneasily, that we ought to be talking about it. It was well enough, I guessed, to have hidden all the facts of love in this impenetrable caul of reticence all one's life, but we were grown women now and she was dying. Could we not even talk of that? Yet neither of us ever spoke. And once again, as I think back on it, it scarcely matters. What could we have said?

At first her self-control was hard won: her face often had a desperate look about it, and she would weep and then stop weeping without offering any explanation. But then she got control again, and the control eventually turned into serenity. Only once, in the final months, did I see it break. She awoke one morning in November and asked what date it was. It happened to be my birthday, and for reasons that I did not immediately understand, she began to cry. "Don't worry, Mother," I kept saying, bewildered. "I don't care if it's my birthday. You don't have to give me a present. . . ."

That only made things worse, and then it dawned on me. Long ago she had made the revolutionary decision to have only one child, or at least not to have twelve children and then turn them into farmhands. So as she lay on her death bed, the event mattered to her. She was not crying because it was my birthday, she was crying because years before, on that same morning, she had been twenty-one and had had a baby. Now, in so short a time, a bewildered young woman stood beside her, hoping to distract her from thoughts of death. I had assumed, as always, that her concern was for me. But she was grieving for another young woman. The tears had nothing to do with me.

Shirley Abbott

208

It was the long fight for life once more.

Once again we carried her on coolies' backs up the mountains to the stone cottage, a bone-thin, indomitable creature, her young and changeless dark eyes looking bravely out of the small face under the mass of white hair.

Once more she set herself bravely to the curing of her body. It was a good body, sound in heritage, but it had been made to respond too often to rally now to her will. It became evident that it would not rally again. She knew it well, and there was a short period, a matter of a few days, when we beheld the spectacle of a young and brave spirit viewing with anger and dismay the old and feeble body which must die. She spoke no word to anyone beyond the courteous words of necessity, but the look of her eyes was terrible, and we turned away in agony at what we saw there.

Then it was over. She accepted it. It was as though she gave her body up then as negligible and worth nothing to her, and she set herself to fulfil the desires of her spirit during the last months. Not that she ever spoke of death. She did not, ignoring the whole matter, and dwelling more than ever upon the beauty she loved above every other part of her life. She spoke often of the sweetness of the bird calls in the trees about the house, of the green shadows on the grass, of the splendor of the lilies on the terrace. At sunset she lay quite still and let her eyes range over the clouds and the vista of the valleys....

Sometimes in the deep night when the darkness pressed upon her and she grew faint and breathless, she turned her enormous eyes toward Comfort who was with her and she asked the old question her own mother had asked, "Child— is this—*death?*"

And when Comfort cried out passionately, "I will not let you

209

die!" she smiled and said, "How like me you are—so I told my mother, too."

One day she said, "There are so many things I have not heard of or seen—so many pleasures. Not one of you knows how I love pleasure! I want a victrola. I want to hear music of all the kinds I have not heard."

We sent to the coast for a victrola and for records and she lay listening by the hour. What she thought I do not know, only she would have no mournful music. Once someone put on the record, "O rest in the Lord, Wait patiently for Him," and she said with a quiet and profound bitterness, "Take that away. I have waited and patiently—for nothing."

We never played it again and to this day I cannot endure that music for the memory it brings back of her voice—not a sorrowful voice, but quiet, proud, resigned, courageous. She had faced by this time the truth, that the search for God with which she had begun her life was not in her time to be fulfilled. . . .

Only once she mentioned her death. She came out of her sleep suddenly and said with great distinctness to Comfort who happened to be the one watching then, "Child, if I should seem afraid at the end, it will be only because this old body of mine takes advantage of me for the moment. It has always been my enemy—always trying to beat me down. You just remember my spirit goes on straight. *I am not afraid!*"

Again she roused herself after that, this time to give directions regarding her tombstone. There were to be no words of commendation, no mention of wifehood or motherhood, only her own name and under that three texts, to be written in English and Chinese also, the last one that triumphant announcement, "To him that overcometh a crown of life shall be given."

Once more she roused herself to say, "Do not sing any sad hymns over me. I want the Glory Song. I hate to die. My life is unfinished. I was going to live to a hundred. But if I must die—I'll die with joy and triumph—I'll go on somehow—"

There were no last words or any sign. She died in her sleep.

Pearl Buck

Old Mother turns blue and from us
   "Don't let my head drop to the earth.
I'm blind and deaf."   Death from the heart,
   a thimble in her purse.

"It's a long day since last night.
   Give me space.   I need
floors.   Wash the floors, Lorine!—
   wash clothes!   Weed!"

Lorine Niedecker

She's dying. Mother is dying! I tried to think, to make myself
realize that Mother, with all this dumb sorrow gazing at me,
was passing, passing away, for ever. But above the dull pain
that pressed on my heart, thinking was impossible. I felt I was
in the clutch of some unreal dream from which I was trying
to waken. Tiny fragments of memory rushed through my mind.
I remembered with what wild abandon Mother had danced
the *kozatzkeh* at a neighbour's wedding. With what passion
she had bargained at the pushcart over a penny.... How her
face lit up whenever company came! How her eyes sparkled
with friendliness as she served the glasses of tea, spread
everything we had on the table, to show her hospitality. A new
pair of stockings, a clean apron, a mere car ride, was an event
in her life that filled her with sunshine for the whole day....
Is there a God over us and sees her suffer so?...She had
seized me by the hand. She had begged me to come and see
her. And I had answered her, "I can come to see you later,
but I can't go to college later..."

"Mamma—mamma!"

Suddenly the sorrowful eyes became transfigured with light.
Her lips moved. I could not get the words, but the love-light
of Mother's eyes flowed into mine. I felt literally Mother's soul
enter my soul like a miracle. Then all became dark.

Anzia Yezierska

For three days and nights I watched by her bedside. A movement
would awaken me as I dozed. Her blue-black eyes were tender
as they followed me back and forth. The doctor who made his
weekly rounds from mining town to mining town was out of
patience ... there seemed nothing wrong with her as he could
see. Yes—pains in the stomach, of course ... that was from
bad food and from too little ... what else could you expect,

he said, if she insisted on living on potatoes and flour-and-water gravy! She must have better food . . . she was under-nourished. I wondered what "under-nourished" could mean. No, he answered my question, even if she wanted it, she could have no more bicarbonate of soda to ease the pain.

During the first two days she talked with me. Annie had died two weeks before . . . that she had written me. She had gone to her, away down on the desolate plain of western Oklahoma where Annie and Sam worked like animals on their homestead. Annie had left the baby . . . a tiny thing, lying in the next room. I warmed milk and fed it, and it watched me with wistful blue eyes; strange it was that its coming should have caused my sister's death.

My mother was very happy as I sat by her. But I think she knew that death was near, for she said strange things to me—things touching the emotions that she would never have dared say otherwise, for affection between parents and children was never shown among my people. She called me "my daughter"—a thing she had never said before in her life.

"I don't know how I could of lived till now if it hadn't been fer you," she said once, as if the words were wrung from her.

Once in the middle of the night she woke me to say: "Promise me you'll go on an' git a better edjication." Her hand closed upon mine, steady and strong, as if asking for a pledge. . . . I clasped her hand . . . Standing by my mother's bedside, I realized that we faced death alone . . . and that I was helpless. . . .

My mother's eyes were large and glistening, and she turned them on me in an appeal beyond all speech. I bent over the bed and, for the first time in my life, took her in my arms and held her close to my trembling body. "Marie!" My name was the last word she ever uttered.

Agnes Smedley

Somebody reached for the clock, while Mrs. Mattie Clarke put her hand to the pillow to take it away.

"Don't!" I cried out. "Don't take the pillow from under Mama's head! She said she didn't want it moved!"

I made to stop Mrs. Mattie, but Papa pulled me away. Others were trying to silence me. I could see the huge drop of sweat collected in the hollow at Mama's elbow and it hurt me so. They were covering the clock and mirror.

"Don't cover up that clock! Leave that looking-glass like it is! Lemme put Mama's pillow back where it was!"

But Papa held me tight and the others frowned me down. Mama was still rasping out the last morsel of her life. I think she was trying to say something, and I think she was trying to speak to me. What was she trying to tell me? What wouldn't I give to know! Perhaps she was telling me that it was better for the pillow to be moved so that she could die easy, as they said. Perhaps she was accusing me of weakness and failure in carrying out her last wish. I do not know. I shall never know.

Just then, Death finished his prowling through the house on his padded feet and entered the room. He bowed to Mama in his way, and she made her manners and left us to act out our ceremonies over unimportant things. . . .

But life picked me up from the foot of Mama's bed, grief, self-despisement and all, and set my feet in strange ways. That moment was the end of a phase in my life. I was old before my time with grief of loss, of failure, and of remorse. No matter what the others did, my mother had put her trust in me. She had felt that I could and would carry out her wishes, and I had not. And then in that sunset time, I failed her. It seemed as she died that the sun went down on purpose to flee away from me.

214

That hour began my wanderings. Not so much in geography, but in time. Then not so much in time as in spirit.

Mama died at sundown and changed a world. That is, the world which had been built out of her body and her heart.

Zora Neale Hurston

Harriot Stanton Blatch, worthy daughter of this splendid mother [Elizabeth Cady Stanton], writes me of her last hours: "None of us knew mother was so near her end 'til Sunday really (the day she died). She had been suffering from shortness of breath lately, from time to time, and from that cause felt under the mark. On Saturday she said to the doctor, very emphatically, 'Now, if you can't cure this difficulty of breathing, and if I am not to feel brighter and more like work again, I want you to give me something to send me pack-horse speed to heaven.'...Two hours before her death (on Sunday) she said she wished to stand up....The trained nurse...and the doctor...helped her to rise and stood on either side of her....She drew herself up very erect (the doctor said the muscular strength was extraordinary) and there she stood for seven or eight minutes, steadily looking out, proudly before her. I think she was mentally making an address. When we urged her to sit down she fell asleep....She slipped away peacefully in a few minutes."... I can see her now, standing there in her last hours, with that delicate halo of soft, white curls around her death-touched face, pleading once again the cause of the mothers of the race, before an imaginary audience of sons and fathers of those who have lost in her their most eloquent, far-reaching voice.

For in her the world has lost its greatest woman, its noblest mother, its clearest thinker. She embraced in her motherhood all who were under the ban of oppression; she thought for the thoughtless of whatever sex; she was great enough to be honest with her own soul, and to walk in the light of the sun, hand in hand with the naked Truth! And in this she stood almost alone. *Helen Gardener*

1

2

3

4

5

6

7

8

9

10

11

12

13

14

15

16

17

18

19

20

21

SEPTEMBER

22

23

24

25

26

27

28

29

30

OCTOBER
Mournings, Elegies, Tributes

Mama, Shiphra, O my maminke
Cynthia Ozick

My little Mother, my star, my courage, my *own*.
Katherine Mansfield

Her dying feels to me like many kinds of Cold—at times electric, at
times benumbing—then a trackless waste Love has never trod.
Emily Dickinson

Everything for her, everything, all
poems, all movings up, all goodnesses,
everything begging, begging, Mama, Mama
of Magic, forgive.   Forgive.   Forgive.
Lucille Clifton

My twin, my sister, my lost love.
Marge Piercy

It's still inside me

like that ninety-pound fibroid tumor
in that woman's womb.

It took two doctors to lift it out of her,
the paper said.

But who will help me.
                              Judith Hemschemeyer

She has withdrawn from us.
A small mound blurs
the angled line of bed.
A woman older than her years
lies waiting for release,
her worn face carved
from early softness
into scraps of wire and flesh.

Unused to rest, her hands
lie quiet on the spread,
their veins reveal
a pulse each hour more secret.
At last flow falters,
ebbs beyond our tracing.

The vigil ends. Footsteps
descend the stairs, dislodge
white powder from a ceiling crack.
It sifts through sunlight,
drifts, and settles on a cat
caught in an eye of light.

Neighbors arrive. Set covered
dishes on the table
where hired hands had nattered
over crops and cows and endless meals,
then one by one approach the man
who sits, a weathered bull past prime.
Speak in hushed voices of a woman
they assumed they knew, who ran
a treadmill to and fro from that board.

Retreating to the sink, I slosh
wet busy work. Clutch at her clumsy
bar of home-made soap, and see
her lye scarred hands as I had
come upon them once at early dawn,
kneading great lumps of dough.
Naming each yeasty rising mound
his name, and pounding, pounding....

Before me on the narrow sill
her meager plants bend toward the light.
A movement in the window calls my eyes
The rooster struts, trails from his spurs
a slime of unborn life and broken shell.
Above, against the morning sky a sharp
calligraphy of small swift wings take flight.

Maude Meehan

Mama, lying so far down,
the earth is your womb now.
Your children stand
over your grave,
                        your mother.

Your blood is alive,
a river in our veins.
We are rain swelling oceans,
Pouring over this grave,
                        your womb.

The earth cradles you now.
We listen to the wind.
It is your voice
and heartbeat
as you held us each
against your breast....

Our windows
won't bring you back,
though we press against them,
aching for headlights
to turn into our driveway.

On the wind
your voice sweeps the clouds,
black and rain-heavy.
We are bursting
out of our womb,
                    your grave.
                    Hilary Sametz Lloyd

O my mother,
now you know everything unendingly—
know too the place where the end of the way
was torn in flames
from the prophets' bodies.

And Esau's tear
wept into
the hide of defeat.

And the mist-bud
of melancholy in the blood.

O my mother,
now you know everything unendingly—
know too the Milky Way's ragged wonders
of dreams and signs.

And what is released
from the open wound of your breath!

Oh my mother,
now you know everything unendingly—
for Rachel's grave has long since turned to music—
and stone and sand
a breath in the sea,
and cradle song from all the stars:
rise in the fall—

And borders everywhere of sea—

you know—

Nelly Sachs

Before I slept, I saw the nebula
of your ashes swirl in the sea
and smash into stars on the sand.
For hours after I hunted the shore
listening for your voice in shells
that went mute in my hand.
When I begged the sea for your face
the fog came in.

Now you surface in my sleep.
Hoarse cries sound in the bay of my ear.
You chip my eyes with rock
and lids split open like mussel shells.
I see you floating on the swell
and spill, crowned with kelp
and sleek as the sea itself
you preen and dive and glide.
I am honored beyond song.

Katherine Doak

from Emily Dickinson's letters

To Mrs. J. Howard Sweetser   *November 1882*
Dear Nellie,

... Wondering with sorrow, how we could spare our lost Neighbors, our first Neighbor, our Mother, quietly stole away.

So unobtrusive was it, so utterly unexpected, that she almost died with Vinnie alone before one could be called. Amid these foreign Days the thought of you is homelike, for you were peculiarly gentle to her for whom service has ceased ....

Plundered of her dear face, we scarcely know each other, and feel as if wrestling with a Dream, waking would dispel ....

Oh, Vision of Language!

To Louise and Frances Norcross   *late November 1882*
Dear cousins,

I hoped to write you before, but mother's dying almost stunned my spirit.

I have answered a few inquiries of love, but written little intuitively. She was scarcely the aunt you knew. The great mission of pain had been ratified–cultivated to tenderness by persistent sorrow, so that a larger mother died than had she died before. There was no earthly parting. She slipped from our fingers like a flake gathered by the wind, and is now part of the drift called "the infinite."

We don't know where she is, though so many tell us . . . .

I cannot tell how Eternity seems. It sweeps around me like a sea . . . . Thank you for remembering me. Remembrance— mighty word.

To Mrs. J. G. Holland   *mid-December 1882*
Dear Sister.

I have thought of you with confiding Love, but to speak seemed taken from me–Blow has followed blow, till the wondering terror of the Mind clutches what is left, helpless of an accent. . . .

Mother has now been gone five Weeks. We should have thought it a long Visit, were she coming back–Now the "Forever" thought almost shortens it, as we are nearer rejoining her than her own return–We were never intimate Mother and Children while she was our Mother–but Mines in the same Ground meet by tunneling and when she became our Child, the Affection came–When we were Children and she journeyed, she always brought us something. Now, would she bring us but herself, what an only Gift–Memory is a strange Bell-Jubilee, and Knell . . . .

Is God Love's Adversary?

To Maria Whitney   *spring 1883*
Dear Friend,

. . . All is faint indeed without our vanished mother, who achieved in sweetness what she lost in strength, though grief of wonder at her fate made the winter short, and each night I reach finds my lungs more breathless, seeking what it means . . . .

> Fashioning what she is,
> Fathoming what she was,
> We deem we dream–
> And that dissolves the days
> Through which existence strays
> Homeless at home.

Emily (Dickinson)

> The Work of Her that went,
> The Toil of Fellows done–
> In Ovens green our Mother bakes,
> By Fires of the Sun.

Emily Dickinson

May 19, 6 p.m. Now it is May 1919. Six o'clock. I am sitting in my own room thinking of Mother: I want to cry. But my thoughts are beautiful and full of gaiety. I think of *our* house, *our* garden, *us* children—the lawn, the gate, and Mother coming in. "Children! Children!" I really only ask for time to write it all—time to write my books. Then I don't mind dying. I live to write. The lovely world (God, how lovely the external world is!) is there and I bathe in it and am refreshed. But I feel as though I had a DUTY, someone has set me a task which I am bound to finish. Let me finish it: let me finish it without hurrying—leaving all as fair as I can . . . .

My little Mother, my star, my courage, my *own*. I seem to dwell in her now.   *Katherine Mansfield*

In the March winds my mother comes to me . . . .
In braided red yarn she flies,
no wings, no gold teeth,
eyebrows penciled a fine line.
Her feet grip this brown earth.
She might be sixteen.

Eight years ago I sat with my mother,
sixtyfive, at her blue formica table
in her fifth floor apartment . . . .

How lucky, how lucky
to be born in America,
how she was born too soon,
how her luck clouded
beneath the stars,
how it had been decreed
through precepts, through rituals
she would work to bone.

How she insisted
I listen to her very words;
how I closed my ears thinking:
She is only my mother.

And now rainclouds overhead
move like a serpent
breathing fire
into my fingers, piercing my heart.

Nellie Wong

I did not weep my father,
The rich, the fulfilled years . . . .

My heart broke for my mother.
I buried grief with her.

It is the incomplete,
The unfulfilled, the torn
That haunts our nights and days
And keeps us hunger-born . . . .

There are some griefs so loud
They could bring down the sky,
And there are griefs so still
None knows how deep they lie,
Endured, never expended.
There are old griefs so proud
They never speak a word;
They never can be mended.
And these nourish the will
And keep it iron-hard.

May Sarton

Since my mother's death I've been holding on, clinging desperately to her and to a youthful version of myself. Losing her physical being, her force, her umbrage, seemed a maiming, even an annihilation, of my own existence. She was the *mysterium tremendum* of life.

But that season is over.

Slowly I find myself being weaned from her material presence. Yet, filled with her as never before. It is I now who represent us both. I am our mutual past. I am my mother and my self. She gave me love, to love myself, and to love the world. I must remember how to love.

Piece by piece, I reenter the world. A new phase. A new body, a new voice. Birds console me by flying, trees by growing, dogs by the warm patch they leave behind on the sofa. Unknown people merely by performing their motions.... Gone is that pinch-penny effort to accordion each calendar day. Time is a gift rather than a goad. Diminished is concern about people's opinions, abandoned the notion of perfection, the illusion that children can be spared grief and disappointment.

I knew a beautiful woman once. And she was my mother. I knew a tenderness once. And it was my mother's. Oh, how happy I was to be loved.

And now I mourn her. I mourn that cornerstone. I mourn her caring. I mourn the one who always hoped for me. I mourn her lost image of me. The lost infant in myself. My lost happiness. I mourn my own eventual death. My life now is only mine....

Every blade, every leaf, every seed in my portion of the world has shifted. Your presence hovers everywhere, over house, over garden, over dreams, over silence. You are within me. I'll not lose you.

Once I was born. Can I be born again? Oh, wean me from pain to love. Help me to use your love and strength in my own life. Help me to carry my world.   *Toby Talbot*

1

2

3

4

5

6

7

8

9

10

11

12

13

14

15

16

17

18

19

20

21

22

23

24

25

26

27

28

29

30

31

NOVEMBER
Legacies
(As Is This All)

I am the earth, I am the root
Judith Wright

This book by any yet unread,
I leave for you when I am dead,
That being gone, here you may find
What was your living mother's mind.
Make use of what I leave in Love,
And God shall bless you from above.
Anne Bradstreet, c. 1650

In memory of my mother

*She
    somersaulted
        into a golden curve*

*In
    the circle
        was a plague
            of fire*

*Its arc
    was brilliant
        with anger*

*And its edges
    hot
        with pain*

*Out
    of the circle
        I flew . . .*

*I saw
    the fruit
        lying there*

243

Tempting
  in pain
    and pleasure

More bitter
  than sweet
    Then

Future passed
  through her
    and she was the chrysalis

Who gave me the gift of wings

Joyce Carol Thomas

A ship
A chain
A distant land

A whip
A pain
A white man's hand

A sack
A stove
A cornhusk bed

Couldn't bend Grea'gra'ma's back
Never lowered Gra'ma's head.
Sherley Anne Williams

"Isie, Ah ain't goin' tuh be wid yuh much longer, and when Ahm dead Ah wants you tuh have dis bed. Iss mine. Ah sewed fuh uh white woman over in Maitland and she gimme dis bedstead fuh mah work. Ah wants you tuh have it. Dis mah feather tick on here too."

"Yes'm mama. Ah—"

"Stop cryin', Isie, you can't hear whut Ahm sayin', 'member tuh git all de education you kin. Dat's de onliest way you kin keep out from under people's feet. You always strain tuh be de bell cow, never be de tail uh nothin'. Do de best you kin, honey, 'cause neither yo' paw nor dese older chillun is goin' tuh be bothered too much wid yuh, but you goin' tuh git 'long. Mark mah words. You got de spunk, but mah po' li'l' sandy-haired chile goin' suffer uh lot 'fo' she git tuh de place she kin 'fend fuh herself. And Isie, honey, stop cryin' and lissen tuh me. Don't you love nobody better'n you do yo'self. Do, you'll be dying befo' yo' time is out. And, Isie, uh person kin be killed 'thout being stuck uh blow. Some uh dese things Ahm tellin' yuh, you won't understand 'em fuh years tuh come, but de time will come when you'll know."

Zora Neale Hurston

This old woman . . .
isn't my mother,   is not
what I think. She's a spiritual
master   trying to teach me
how to carry my soul lightly
how to make each step an important journey,
every motion and breath   anywhere
as though anywhere were the center of earth.

Betsy Sholl

NOVEMBER

Housework, sewing, customers: how, when you have your work always in your hands, do you keep four children from straying? ... She kept us on the long leash of an endless rope of language, looping and knotting us as firmly to her as ever she stitched edge to edge in a seam. She lassoed us daily and webbed us and gilded our lives with innumerable threads of prose. Words spun about us; sometimes the very air was afog with words that purled like a fine mist about our ears: stories and persuasions and fantasies and cajolings and adjurations and just plain fast-talking that fogged up your brain with ideas, intoxicated you, led you half hypnotized where she wanted you to go. Like a conjurer she kept us busy, kept us interested, kept us occupied, kept us fascinated, winding us in endless strings of reciprocal talk, ropes of argument, singing necklaces, bracelets of laughter, looping us with garments of language, bejewelling us with glittering sentences, bubbling and streaming ideas and thoughts and discussion and exhortations and moralizings, and sometimes, when we'd briefly slipped the spell, an anxious crying of our names up and down the block, or a stern motherly shout or two ....

Not until I heard her with her grandchildren did I remember the feeling of it, those invisible, constantly re-forming bonds which at the same time were roads to explore, teasing us along avenues of thought and imagination ....

Mind you, even as a child you knew you were being led, and as you grew older you sometimes suspected you were being taken, but who could resist? Who wanted to miss anything? You knew she was building a glittering web to contain you but you knew you were always at its centre, and it was a throne, a chariot, as it became a rocket ship for her grandchildren, perhaps, and she might be controlling you but she was also completely at your service, helping you learn to work

246

the controls that would take you farther, she promised, than even her dreams. She was artist, magician, slave and seer, counsellor, songbird, judge and peer.   *Adele Wiseman*

I learned from the age of two or three that any room in our house, at any time of day, was there to read in, or to be read to. My mother read to me. She'd read to me in the big bedroom in the mornings, when we were in her rocker together, which ticked in rhythm as we rocked, as though we had a cricket accompanying the story. She'd read to me in the diningroom on winter afternoons in front of the coal fire, with our cuckoo clock ending the story with "Cuckoo," and at night when I'd got in my own bed. I must have given her no peace. Sometimes she read to me in the kitchen while she sat churning, and the churning sobbed along with *any* story.

She could still recite [the poems in McGuffey's Readers] in full when she was lying helpless and nearly blind, in her bed, an old lady. Reciting, her voice took on resonance and firmness, it rang with the old fervor, with ferocity even. She was teaching me one more, almost her last, lesson: emotions do not grow old. I knew that I would feel as she did, and I do.

Eudora Welty

My mother is a poem I'll never be able to write
though everything I write is a poem to my mother . . . .
I don't know why she is hard to find.
She has given me all the stories.
She is the story line of this poem. My mother, my
    optimist . . . .

The Cherokee, Choctaw and Seminole
buried their dead infants
as the boundary lines of their nations.
My mother settled into the nations of Mother
with the same unconditional allegiance.

She had three babies in three years.
Flowers became her escape.
I looked out the window once
saw her lie down in their bed.

My mother is a poem I'll never write.
In her as John Muir says
one may think the clouds themselves
are plants . . . .

o, wild girl of the river I named my son for. *Mother,
Father. Brother. Sister. Daughter. Country*.
She summons them out of the flowers and stones,
on the road disappearing around the hill,
down the tracks of the one who was lost.
She hunts them to where the sea begins.
She rides a runaway horse through this poem,
a strange opium through my blood.
She tells me the stories, a search
for the living, a hidden road

out from
all the known places.

This is a poem that cannot end

Sharon Doubiago

DEDICATIONS

for
Elvira Moraga Lawrence and
Mamalia Garcia Anzaldua
and for all our mothers
for the obedience and rebellion
they taught us.

This Bridge Called My Back

To Mother Thelma
For whipping some
sense in me with
her love

Sturdy Black Bridges

to my first friend, teacher, map maker, landscape aide
Mama
Helen Brent Henderson Cade Brehon
who in 1948, having come upon me daydreaming in the middle
of the kitchen floor, mopped around me.

The Salt Eaters

249

Interviewer: Who has influenced your writing?

My mama. She did *The New York Times* and *The London Times* crossword puzzles. She read books. She built bookcases. She'd wanted to be a journalist. She gave me permission to wonder, to dawdle, to daydream. My most indelible memory of 1948 is my mother coming upon me in the middle of the kitchen floor with my head in the clouds and my pencil on the paper and her mopping around me. My mama had been in Harlem during the renaissance. She used to hang out at the Dark Tower, at the Renny, go to hear Countee Cullen, see Langston Hughes over near Mt. Morris Park. She thought it was wonderful that I could write things that almost made some kind of sense. She used to walk me over to Seventh Avenue and 125th Street and point out the shop where J.A. Rogers, the historian, was knocking out books. She used to walk me over to the Speaker's Corner to listen to the folks. Of course, if they were talking "religious stuff," she'd keep on going to wherever we were going: but if they were talking union or race, we'd hang tough on the corner.   *Toni Cade Bambara*

Mama enjoyed bandying words. In fact, there was scarcely anything she enjoyed more. She made up words from scratch, by combining words, by turning them upside down, by running them backward. She built word palaces. Structures came out of her mouth like Steinberg pictures: wobbly, made of material fabricated on the spot, and no more useful than a poem.

When mama talked, the listener lived at the point of Joyce's pen. Like Joyce she used words that didn't exist—but her meanings were clearer than Webster or the *Britannica* ever managed. Mostly she was funny. . . . She gave Him all the praise, but He had given her the ability, the compulsion, to pull a word or a happening askew, to show the world to us as it was, slantwise and si-goglin. *Jessamyn West*

In the week before her death, I, trying to identify myself to her, said, "I'm the oldest of your four children."
"The oldest?" she repeated.
"The one who wrote those Quaker stories." . . .
"Oh," said she, "did I get those stories written?"
"Written and published," I said.
"I always wanted to write them. But I married early and wasn't well. It slipped my mind that I did it. I thought I just dreamed I did it." . . .
What she thought she remembered was purest fiction, something that never happened. What *had* happened, the clink of her mother's wedding ring as she washed dishes, her grandfather's love of music, the whisper of snow, the rustle of shawls and full skirts in the Meetinghouse on First Day: these, the realities of which she told me, had been *my* dreams. . . .
Her memories and long-time musings had become my fiction. *Jessamyn West*

251

No song or poem will bear my mother's name. Yet so many of the stories that I write, that we all write, are my mother's stories. Only recently did I fully realize this: that through the years of listening to my mother's stories of her life, I have absorbed not only the stories themselves, but something of the manner in which she spoke, something of the urgency that involves the knowledge that her stories—like her life—must be recorded....

But the telling of these stories, which came from my mother's lips as naturally as breathing, was not the only way my mother showed herself as an artist. For stories, too, were subject to being distracted, to dying without conclusion. Dinners must be started, and cotton must be gathered before the big rains....

Like Mem, a character in *The Third Life Of Grange Copeland*, my mother adorned with flowers whatever shabby house we were forced to live in.... Whatever she planted grew as if by magic, and her fame as a grower of flowers spread over three counties. Because of her creativity with her flowers, even my memories of poverty are seen through a screen of blooms—sunflowers, petunias, roses, dahlias, forsythia, spirea, delphiniums, verbena... and on and on....

I notice that it is only when my mother is working in her flowers that she is radiant, almost to the point of being invisible—except as Creator: hand and eye. She is involved in work her soul must have. Ordering the universe in the image of her personal conception of Beauty.

Her face, as she prepares the Art that is her gift, is a legacy of respect she leaves to me, for all that illuminates and cherishes life. She had handed down respect for the possibilities—and the will to grasp them.

For her, so hindered and intruded upon in so many ways, being an artist has still been a daily part of her life.

Alice Walker

252

My mother's death unveiled and intensified; made me suddenly develop perceptions, as if a burning glass had been laid over what was shaded and dormant . . . as if something were becoming visible without any effort. . . . I had a feeling of transparency in words when they cease to be words and become so intensified that one seems to experience them; to foretell them as if they developed what one is already feeling. I was so astonished that I tried to explain the feeling. "One seems to understand what it's about," I said awkwardly. I suppose Nessa has forgotten; no one could have understood from what I said the queer feeling I had in the hot grass, that poetry was coming true. Nor does that give the feeling—it matches what I have sometimes felt when I write.   *Virginia Woolf*

Whenever I feel myself inferior to everything about me, threatened by my own mediocrity, frightened by the discovery that a muscle is losing its strength, a desire its power. or a pain the keen edge of its bite, I can still hold up my head and say to myself. . . . "I am the daughter of a woman who, in a mean, close-fisted, confined little place, opened her village home to stray cats, tramps, and pregnant servant girls. I am the daughter of a woman who many a time, when she was in despair at not having enough money for others, ran through the wind-whipped snow to cry from door to door, at the houses of the rich, that a child had just been born in a poverty-stricken home to parents whose feeble, empty hands had no swaddling clothes for it. Let me not forget that I am a daughter of a woman who bent her head, trembling, between the blades of a cactus, her wrinkled face full of ecstasy over the promise of a flower, a woman who herself never ceased to flower, untiringly, during three quarters of a century."   *Colette*

1

2

3

4

5

6

7

8

9

10

11

12

13

14

15

16

17

18

19

20

21

22

23

24

25

26

27

28

29

30

DECEMBER
The Larger Caring: Dream-Visions

To
a small girl child
who may live to grasp
somewhat of that which for
us
is yet sight, not touch.
Olive Schreiner

"Mama . . . Oh why is it like it is and why do I have to care?"
Caressing, quieting. Thinking: *caring asks doing. It is a long baptism into the seas of humankind, my daughter. Better immersion than to live untouched. . . . Yet how will you sustain?*   *Tillie Olsen*

[My mother's] voice that on that day and on all the other days spoke words that had always the same meaning: "The child must have proper care. Can't we save that woman? Have those people got enough to eat? I can hardly kill that creature."   *Colette*

I'm alive to want more than life
want it for others starving and unborn.
Adrienne Rich

i would be a fool to want more children.
why do my arms feel open.
so that all the children
walk into their circle.
why are my arms so open
to the weeping girl on the bus,
her tears on my breast.
why do i have enuf love
to wish all our children well.
why do the children
approach me without fear.

Alta

DREAM-VISION

In the winter of 1955, in her last weeks of life, my mother—
so much of whose waking life had been a nightmare, that
common everyday nightmare of hardship, limitation, longing;
of baffling struggle to raise six children in a world hostile to
human unfolding—my mother, dying of cancer, had beautiful
dream-visions—in color.

Already beyond calendar time, she could not have known
that the last dream she had breath to tell came to her on
Christmas Eve. Nor, conscious, would she have named it so.
As a girl in long ago Czarist Russia, she had sternly broken
with all observances of organized religion, associating it with
pogroms and wars; "mind forg'd manacles"; a repressive state.
We did not observe religious holidays in her house.

Perhaps, in her last consciousness, she *did* know that the
year was drawing towards that solstice time of the shortest
light, the longest dark, the cruellest cold, when—as she had

261

explained to us as children—poorly sheltered ancient peoples in northern climes had summoned their resources to make out of song, light, food, expressions of human love—festivals of courage, hope, warmth, belief.

It seemed to her that there was a knocking at her door. Even as she rose to open it, she guessed who would be there, for she heard the neighing of camels. (I did not say to her: "Ma, camels don't neigh.") Against the frosty lights of a far city she had never seen, "a city holy to three faiths," she said, the three wise men stood: magnificent in jewelled robes of crimson, of gold, of royal blue.

"Have you lost your way?" she asked, "Else, why do you come to me? I am not religious, I am not a believer."

"To talk with *you*, we came," the wise man whose skin was black and robe crimson, assured her, "to talk of whys, of wisdom."

"Come in then, come in and be warm—and welcome. I have starved for such talk."

But as they began to talk, she saw that they were not men, but women:

That they were not dressed in jewelled robes, but in the coarse everyday shifts and shawls of the old country women of her childhood, their feet wrapped round and round with rags for lack of boots; snow now sifting into the room;

That their speech was not highflown, but homilies; their bodies not lordly in bearing, magnificent, but stunted, misshapen—used all their lives as a beast of burden is used;

That the camels were not camels, but farm beasts, such as were kept in the house all winter, their white cow breaths steaming into the cold.

And now it was many women, a babble.

One old woman, seamed and bent, began to sing. Swaying, the others joined her, their faces and voices transfiguring as they sang; my mother, through cracked lips, singing too—a lullaby.

For in the shining cloud of their breaths, a baby lay, breathing the universal sounds every human baby makes, sounds out of which are made all the separate languages of the world.

Singing, one by one the women cradled and sheltered the baby.

"The joy, the reason to believe," my mother said, "the hope for the world, the baby, holy with possibility, that is all of us at birth." And she began to cry, out of the dream and its telling now.

"Still I feel the baby in my arms, the human baby," crying now so I could scarcely make out the words, "the human baby, before we are misshapen; crucified into a sex, a color, a walk of life, a nationality . . .and the world yet warrings and winter.

I had seen my mother but three times in my adult life, separated as we were by the continent between, by lack of means, by jobs I had to keep and by the needs of my four children. She could scarcely write English—her only education in this country a few months of night school. When at last I flew to her, it was in the last days she had language at all. Too late to talk with her of what was in our hearts; or of harms and crucifying and strengths as she had known and experienced them; or of whys and knowledge, of wisdom. She died a few weeks later.

She, who had no worldly goods to leave, yet left to me an inexhaustible legacy. Inherent in it, this heritage of summoning resources to make—out of song, food, warmth, expressions of human love—courage, hope, resistance, belief; this vision of universality, before the lessenings, harms, divisions of the world are visited upon it.

She sheltered and carried that belief, that wisdom—as she sheltered and carried us, and others—throughout a lifetime lived in a world whose season was, as still it is, a time of winter.   *Tillie Olsen*

The whole weight of history bears down
on the awful mother's shoulders.
Hiroshima, the Holocaust, the Inquisition
each massacre of innocents
her own childhood
and the childhood of her mother
and the childhood of her child.
What can she do?
She remembers.
The child's drawing, the lost
mittens, the child
cold, the awful mother shouting
the child's story of shadows
in her room, the child waiting
the awful mother
waiting, and *her* mother
waiting, already asleep
and the awful mother
knowing too late
the howling of children
in cattle cars and fires.
The wind blows so hard
it is as if the earth had fallen
on its side.

But nobody wakes up.
Only the awful mother stirs stricken
with grief.

Susan Griffin

Again . . . have the skill and power of two great nations exhausted themselves in mutual murder. Again have the sacred questions of international justice been committed to the fatal mediation of military weapons. . . . [Again] the ambition of rulers has been allowed to barter the dear interests of domestic life for the bloody exchanges of the battle-field. Thus men have done. Thus men will do. But women need no longer be made a party to proceedings which fill the globe with grief and horror. Despite the assumptions of physical force, the mother has a sacred and commanding word to say to the sons who owe their life to her suffering. That word should now be heard, and answered to as never before.

Arise, then, Christian women of this day! Arise, all women who have hearts, whether your baptism be that of water or of tears! Say firmly: "We will not have great questions decided by irrelevant agencies. . . . Our sons shall not be taken from us to unlearn all that we have been able to teach them of charity, mercy and patience. We, women of one country, will be too tender of those of another country, to allow our sons to be trained to injure theirs. From the bosom of the devastated earth a voice goes up with our own. It says: "Disarm, Disarm! . . ."

Let [us] solemnly take counsel with each other as to the means whereby the great human family can live in peace [and there be] amicable settlement of international questions.

Julia Ward Howe, from "An Appeal to Womanhood Throughout the World," 1870

Child of hope, child of promise. It was a time (like now) when death seemed imminent. The world of bomb shelters, weapons, madness lurked behind each newspaper page, and shouted drunkenly from radios and T.V. I refused to read them and would not listen.... The world stayed with us, though I tried to hide.... Still I couldn't help overhearing the talk of Cuba and the Bay of Pigs and the Kennedy ultimatum and the Soviet reply.There came a night...when an early storm came across the Pacific and battered the city where we lived. The rain had been heavy and the winds were ferocious. I woke from a deep sleep to the sound of a siren, the air-raid alert. I found out later it was a short circuit, a meaningless accident. But that night I did not know. And I believed.

Oh child of life. Child of tomorrow. I come up to your room and stand there in the half-light from the street-lamp. The siren sounds again and is silent. I pick you up, gently, and wrap a blanket against the chill air. We stand there, you and I, body to body. And wait. I believe it is the end. I know this holocaust will take not only you and me, but all the world, all children, all trees and songs, all promises. The sirens have sounded and I believe. Your hands flutter against my bare shoulder. Long-fingered and relaxed, they are made to play music and to paint. I hold you and can do nothing. Nothing to give you tomorrow, nothing to save you, nothing to protect what might be. There is no gesture of defiance, no gallant last battle. Just you and I in this room with the wind and rain against the window.

I stand here holding you and watch your eyelids flutter in your sleep. You have your grandmother's chin, your father's nose. Your eyes have the almond slant of a distant ancestor I never knew. I hold your pulsing wrist to my lips, feel again your struggle to be born, and know I must promise you the

266

only thing I have left. If we live through this night, dear child of my body, if we survive these moments of ultimate madness, I will do what I can to shift the balance. I do not know if we can make a difference. I do not know if this death of life can be held back. But I must do what I can, whatever I can. And if, in the end, we lose, I will look at you, straight at you, and say I tried.

The wind smashes the rain against the window glass. I hold you close and do not weep.

Julie Olsen Edwards

Our own shadows disappear as the feet of thousands
by the tens of thousands pound the fallow land
into new dust that
rising like a marvelous pollen will be
fertile
even as the first woman whispering
imagination to the trees around her made
for righteous fruit
from such deliberate defense of life
as no other still
will claim inferior to any other safety
in the world

The whispers too they
intimate to the inmost ear of every spirit
now aroused they
carousing in ferocious affirmation
of all peaceable and loving amplitude
sound a certainly unbounded heat
from a baptismal smoke where yes
there will be fire

267

DECEMBER

And the babies cease alarm as mothers
raising arms
and heart high as the stars so far unseen
nevertheless hurl into the universe
a moving force
irreversible as light years
traveling to the open
eye

And who will join this standing up
and the ones who stood without sweet company
and sing and sing
back into the mountains and
if necessary
even under the sea

We are the ones we have been waiting for

June Jordan

We mothers,
we gather seed of desire
from oceanic night,
we are gatherers
of scattered goods.

We mothers,
pacing dreamily
with the constellations,
the floods
of past and future,
leave us alone
with our birth
like an island. . . .

We who impel sand to love and bring
a mirroring world to the stars—

We mothers,
who rock in the cradles
the shadowy memories
of creation's day—
the to and fro of each breath
is the melody of our love song.

We mothers
rock into the heart of the world
the melody of peace.

Nelly Sachs

15

16

17

18

19

20

21

22

23

24

25

26

27

28

29

30

31

SOURCES

JANUARY
Mother to Daughter: Her Own Voice

Anne Sexton, excerpts from "The Fortress," *All My Pretty Ones*, Houghton Mifflin, 1962.

Janice Mirikitani, excerpt from "Sing with My Body," *Awake in the River*, Isthmus, 1978.

Michele Murray, excerpts from "Dance Poem," *The Great Mother and Other Poems*, Sheed and Ward, 1974.

Judith Wright, "Woman to Child," *The Double Tree: Selected Poems, 1942–1976*, Houghton Mifflin, 1978.

Susan Griffin, "Rebecca."

Elizabeth Gaskell, "Precepts for the Guidance of a Daughter," *The Letters of Mrs. Gaskell*, ed. by J. A. V. Chapple and Arthur Pollard, Harvard University Press, 1967, Manchester University Press, 1966.

Lady Otomo of Sakanoue, excerpts from "Sent from the Capital to Her Elder Daughter," *Penguin Book of Japanese Verse*, ed. and trans. by Geoffrey Bownas and Anthony Thwaite, Penguin, 1964.

Janice Mirikitani, excerpts from "Sing with My Body."

Maxine Kumin, "The Journey: For Janet at Thirteen," *Our Ground Time Here Will Be Brief*, Viking, 1982.

Jeanne Murray Walker, excerpts from "For My Daughter's Twenty-First Birthday," *Extended Outlooks: The Iowa Review Collection of Contemporary Women Writers*, ed. by Jane Cooper, Macmillan, 1982.

Sharon Olds, "35/10," from lyrics to *The Dead and the Living*, Knopf, 1984.

Harriet Beecher Stowe, *Harriet Beecher Stowe* by Catherine Gilbertson, D. Appleton-Century, 1937; Kennikat Press, 1968.

Rosalie Sorrels, excerpts from lyrics to "Apple of My Eye," *What, Women, and Who, Myself, I Am*, ed. by Rosalie Sorrels, Wooden Shoe, 1974.

Margaret Mead, excerpts from "That I be not a restless ghost," *Blackberry Winter*, William Morrow, 1972; Angus & Robertson, 1981.

Ruth Stone, "Advice," *Topography and Other Poems*, Harcourt Brace Jovanovich, 1971.

275

Sources

Alice Walker, "Foregiveness," *Good Night Willie Lee I'll See You in the Morning,* Dial, 1979.

Kay Keeshan Hamod, excerpts from "Transitions," *Working It Out: 23 Women Writers, Artists, Scientists, and Scholars Talk about Their Lives and Work,* ed. by Sara Ruddick and Pamela Daniels, Random House, 1979.

Carolyn Kizer, excerpts from "The Blessing," *Yin: New Poems,* BOA Editions, 1984.

Michele Murray, excerpts from "Dance Poem."

FEBRUARY
Daughter to Mother

Lucille Clifton, excerpt from "February 13, 1980," *Two-Headed Woman,* University of Massachusetts Press, 1980.

George Eliot, excerpt from *Daniel Deronda,* 1876.

Nelly Sachs, "O My Mother," *The Seeker and Other Poems,* trans. by Ruth and Matthew Mead, Farrar, Straus and Giroux, 1970.

Lucille Clifton, exerpt from "February 13, 1980."

Laurel O. Hoye, "You are . . ."

Marge Piercy, excerpt from "My Mother's Body," *My Mother's Body,* Knopf (forthcoming 1985).

Nellie Wong, excerpt from "Red Journeys."

Adele Wiseman, excerpt from *Old Woman at Play,* Clarke, Irwin, 1978.

Theresa Palma Acosta, excerpt from "My Mother Pieced Quilts," *Festival de Flor y Canto,* University of Southern California Press, n.d.

Judith Sornberger, "Thinking of My Mother Who Fifteen Years Later, Has Gone East to See the Leaves."

Sue Standing, excerpts from "Cellar Door," *Amphibious Weather,* Zephyr, 1981.

Anne Sexton, excerpt from her *Diary.*

Elizabeth Akers Allen, excerpts from "Rock Me to Sleep, Mother," *Rock Me to Sleep, Mother,* Estes and Lauriat, 1884.

Jane Cooper, "My Young Mother," *The Weather of Six Mornings,* Macmillan, 1969.

Marge Piercy, excerpt from "My Mother's Body."

Laura Davis, excerpts from "Things You Gave Me."

Hannah Senesh, "To My Mother," trans. by Ruth Finer Mintz, *Hannah Senesh: Her Life and Diary,* Schocken, 1972.

Nelly Sachs, "O My Mother."

Sources

MARCH
Anger, Chasms, Estrangements

Audre Lorde, excerpt from "Story Books on a Kitchen Table," *Coal*, Norton, 1976.

Stephanie Markman, excerpt from "and/mother why did you tell me," *One Foot on the Mountain*, Onlywomen Press, 1979.

Patricia Cumming, "Ceasura," *Letter from an Outlying Province*, Alicejames-books, 1976.

Audre Lorde, "Story Books on a Kitchen Table."

Laura Davis, excerpts from "Things You Gave Me."

Ai, "But What I'm Trying to Say Mother Is," *Cruelty*, Houghton, 1973.

Alice Munro, excerpt from "Red Dress," *Dance of the Happy Shades*, McGraw-Hill, 1973; Penguin, 1983.

Alice Munro, excerpt from *Lives of Girls and Women*, McGraw-Hill, 1971; Penguin, 1982.

Margaret Laurence, excerpt from *The Diviners*, Knopf, 1974.

Cora Sandel, excerpts from *Krane's Cafe*, Peter Owen, c. 1946.

Shirley Kaufman, "I Hear You," *The Floor Keeps Turning*, University of Pittsburgh Pr., 1970.

Cherrie Moraga, excerpts from "La Dulce Culpa," *Loving in the War Years: Lo Que Nunca Paso por sus Labios*, South End Press, 1983.

Stephanie Markman, excerpt from "and/mother why did you tell me."

Simone de Beauvoir, excerpt from *A Very Easy Death*, trans. by Patrick O'Brian, Putnam, 1965; Penguin, 1969.

Tillie Olsen, excerpt from "Tell Me a Riddle," *Tell Me a Riddle*, Delacorte, 1961; Virago Press, 1980.

APRIL
Healings, Understandings, Intimacies, Shelters

Audre Lorde, excerpt from "Black Mother Woman," *A Land Where Other People Live*, Broadside Press, 1971.

Nellie Wong, excerpt from "From a Heart of Rich Straw," *Dreams in Harrison Railroad Park*, Kelsey Street Press, 1977.

Virginia Woolf, excerpts from *Moments of Being*, Harcourt Brace Jovanovich, 1976; Hogarth Press, 1978; Panther, 1978.

Nancy Hale, excerpts from *Life in the Studio*, Little, Brown, 1969.

Catherine Cookson, excerpts from *Our Kate: An Autobiography*, Bobbs-Merrill Co., Inc., 1971; Corgi, 1974; Macdonald, 1982.

277

Sources

Paule Marshall, excerpts from *Brown Girl, Brownstones*, The Feminist Press, 1981; Virago Press, 1982.

Audre Lorde, "Black Mother Woman."

Michele Murray, excerpt from "Poem of Two," *The Great Mother and Other Poems*, Sheed and Ward, 1974.

Katie McBain, excerpts from "I Want to Be Your Daughter Now."

Celia Gilbert, "Circles," *The Women's Review of Books* 1:8 (May 1984).

Agnes Smedley, excerpts from *Daughter of Earth (1928)*, The Feminist Press, 1973; Virago Press, 1977.

Miriam Khamadi Were, excerpts from *The Eighth Wife*, East African Publishing, 1972.

Louisa May Alcott, excerpt from *Little Women*, Roberts Brothers, 1889; Bantam, 1983.

Tillie Olsen, excerpts from *Yonnondio*, Delacorte, 1974; Faber, 1974; Virago Press, 1980.

Muriel Rukeyser, "Night Feeding," *The Collected Poems of Muriel Rukeyser*, McGraw-Hill, 1979.

Ellen Bass, "There Are Times In Life When One Does the Right Thing," *Our Stunning Harvest*, New Society Publ., 1984.

Mary Gordon, excerpts from *The Company of Women*, Random House, 1980; Jonathan Cape, 1981; Corgi, 1982.

Doris Lessing, excerpts from *The Golden Notebook*, Simon and Schuster, 1962; Michael Joseph, 1972; Panther, 1973.

MAY

Mothering: Some Troublous Contexts

Tillie Olsen, excerpt from *Yonnondio*, Delacorte, 1974; Faber, 1974; Virago Press, 1980.

Gravestone epitaphs, compiled by Tillie Olsen.

Harriet Beecher Stowe, excerpts from *The Life and Letters of Harriet Beecher Stowe*, ed. by Annie Fields, 1970.

Harriet Connor Brown, excerpts from *Grandmother Brown's Hundred Years, 1827–1927*, Little, Brown, 1929.

Mary Austin, excerpts from *A Woman of Genius*, Doubleday, 1912, The Feminist Press, 1985.

Edith Summers Kelley, excerpts from *Weeds* (1923), the Feminist Press, 1982.

Harriette Arnow, excerpts from *The Dollmaker*, Macmillan, 1954.

Buchi Emecheta, excerpts from *The Joys of Motherhood*, George Braziller, 1979; Allison & Busby, 1979.

278

Sources

Margaret Sanger, excerpts from *Margaret Sanger: An Autobiography*, Norton, 1983; Dover Publications, 1972.

Gloria Naylor, excerpts from *The Women of Brewster Street*, Viking, 1982; Hodder & Stoughton, 1983.

Tillie Olsen, excerpts from "I Stand Here Ironing," *Tell Me a Riddle*, Delacorte, 1961; Virago Press, 1980.

Sylvia Plath, "Child," *Winter Trees*, Faber, 1971.

Patricia Cumming, "Spring", *Letter from an Outlying Province*, Alicejamesbooks, 1976.

Laurel Lee, excerpts from *Signs of Spring*, Dutton, 1980; Macmillan, 1980.

Ellen Bass, excerpt from "Our Stunning Harvest," *Our Stunning Harvest and Other Poems*, New Society Publ, 1984.

Tillie Olsen, excerpts from "I Stand Here Ironing," *Tell Me a Riddle*.

JUNE

Mothering: Some Extremities and Meditations

Bryna Bar Oni, excerpt from *The Vapor*, Visual Impact, Inc., 1976.

Adrienne Rich, excerpt from *Of Woman Born: Motherhood as Experience and Institution*, Norton, 1976; Virago Press, 1977.

Henry Handel (Ethel Florence) Richardson, excerpts from *Ultima Thule*, Norton, 1929; Penguin, 1972.

Gwendolyn Brooks, excerpts from "the mother," *The World of Gwendolyn Brooks*, Harper and Row, 1971.

Beth Brant, excerpts from "A Long Story," *A Gathering of Spirit: Writing and Art by North American Indian Women*, ed. by Beth Brant, Sinister Wisdom.

Bryna Bar Oni, excerpts from *The Vapor*.

Julie Olsen Edwards, excerpts from "Motheroath," *Women's Studies Quarterly*, Summer 1984.

Marguerite Duras, extract from an interview, files of Tillie Olsen.

Alta, "I would be a fool to want more children," *Shameless Hussy: Selected Prose and Poetry*, The Crossing Press, 1980.

Grace Paley, excerpts from "Mom," *Esquire*, December 1975.

Adrienne Rich, excerpt from *Of Woman Born: Motherhood as Experience and Institution*, Norton, 1976; Virago Press, 1977.

Sources

JULY

Portraits: In Love and Sometimes Anguish

Emily Dickinson, extract from *The Letters of Emily Dickinson*, ed. by Thomas H. Johnson, Harvard University Press, 1965.

Adele Wiseman, extract from *Old Woman at Play*, Clarke, Irwin, 1978.

Jessamyn West, extract from *Hide and Seek: A Continuing Journey*, Harcourt Brace Jovanovich, 1973.

Colette, extracts from *Earthly Paradise*, Farrar, Straus, 1966; Secker & Warburg, 1966; Penguin, 1974.

Jessamyn West, extract from *Hide and Seek: A Continuing Journey*.

Louise Bogan, extracts from *Journey Around My Room*, Viking, 1980.

Margaret Fuller, extracts from *The Woman and the Myth: Margaret Fuller's Life and Writings*, ed. by Bell Gale Chevigny, The Feminist Press, 1976.

Eve Curie, extracts from *Madame Curie*, Doubleday, 1937; Heinemann, 1938.

Jessamyn West, extract from *Hide and Seek: A Continuing Journey*.

Del Marie Rogers, "Desert," *New Poets: Women*, ed. by Terry Wetherby, Les Femmes/Celestial Arts, 1976.

Laureen Mar, "My Mother, Who Came from China, Where She Never Saw Snow," and "Chinatown 4," *The Third Woman: Minority Women Writers of the United States*, ed. by Dexter Fisher, Houghton, 1980.

Agnes Smedley, *Daughter of Earth* (1928), The Feminist Press, 1973; Virago Press, 1977.

Jana Harris, extracts from "When Mama Came Here as a Gold Panner," *Manhattan as a Second Language and Other Poems*, Harper and Row, 1982.

Marge Piercy, extract from "My Mother's Novel," *The Moon Is Always Female*, Knopf, 1980.

May Stevens, extracts from *Ordinary/Extraordinary*.

Gloria Steinem, extracts from "Ruth's Song (Because She Could Not Sing It)", *Outrageous Acts and Everyday Rebellions*, Holt, 1983; Jonathan Cape, 1984.

Virginia Woolf, extracts from *Moments of Being*, Harcourt Brace Jovanovich, 1976; Hogarth Press, 1976; Panther, 1978.

AUGUST

Other Carers, Tenders: Grandmothers, Mammies, Sisters, Teachers

Paula Gunn Allen, excerpt from "Grandmother," *The Third Woman: Minority Women Writers of the United States*, ed. by Dexter Fisher, Houghton Mifflin, 1980.

Sources

Carolyn Forche, excerpts from "Burning the Tomato Worms," *Gathering of the Tribe*, Yale University Press, 1976.

Lillian Smith, excerpt from *The Journey*, World, 1954.

Paula Gunn Allen, "Grandmother."

Carolyn Forche, excerpts from "Burning the Tomato Worms."

Assata Shakur, excerpts from "Women in Prison: How We Are," *Black Scholar*.

Lillian Smith, excerpt from *The Journey*.

Jessamyn West, excerpts from *Hide and Seek: A Continuing Journey*, Harcourt Brace Jovanovich, 1973.

Alice Munro, excerpts from "Winter Wind," *Something I've Been Meaning to Tell You*, McGraw-Hill, 1974.

Adrienne Rich, "Mary Gravely Jones" from "Grandmothers," *A Wild Patience Has Taken Me This Far: Poems 1978–1981*, Norton, 1981.

Ellen Glasgow, excerpts from *The Woman Within*, Harcourt, 1954.

Adrienne Rich, excerpts from *Of Woman Born: Motherhood as Experience and Institution*, Norton, 1976; Virago Press, 1977.

Lillian Hellman, excerpt from *An Unfinished Woman*, Little, Brown, 1969; Quartet Books, 1977.

Lillian Smith, excerpts from *Killers of the Dream*, Norton, 1961.

Audre Lorde, "Teacher," *From a Land Where Other People Live*, Broadside Press, 1971.

Mary Helen Washington, extract from a radio interview, station KPFA San Francisco.

Sherley Anne Williams, "The Peacock Poems: 1," *The Peacock Poems*, Wesleyan University Press, 1975.

Judith Sornberger, "Thinking of My Mother Who Fifteen Years Later, Has Gone East to See the Leaves."

SEPTEMBER
At the Last

Joanne Greenberg, excerpt from *Season of Delight*.

Emily Dickinson, excerpt from *The Letters of Emily Dickinson*, ed. by Thomas H. Johnson, Harvard University Press, 1965.

Zora Neale Hurston, excerpt from *Dust Tracks on a Road*, from *I Love Myself When I Am Laughing . . . And Then Again When I Am Looking Mean and Impressive*, ed. by Alice Walker, The Feminist Press, 1979; Virago Press, 1986 (forthcoming).

Sources

Kaethe Kollwitz, excerpt from *The Diary and Letters of Kaethe Kollwitz*, ed. by Hans Kollwitz, H. Regnery, 1955.

Dorothy Canfield Fisher, excerpt from *Harvest of Stories*, Harcourt, Brace, 1937.

Tillie Olsen, excerpts from "Tell Me a Riddle," *Tell Me A Riddle*, Delacorte, 1961; Virago Press, 1980.

Colette, excerpts from *Earthly Paradise*, Farrar, Straus and Giroux, 1966; Secker &Warburg, 1966; Penguin 1974.

Kaethe Kollwitz, excerpts from *The Diary and Letters of Kaethe Kollwitz.*

Emily Dickinson, excerpts from *The Letters of Emily Dickinson.*

Shirley Kaufman, excerpts from "Apples," *Gold Country*, University of Pittsburgh Press, 1973.

Marie Ponsot, excerpts from "Nursing: Mother," *Admit Impediment*, Knopf, 1981.

Adeline Naiman, excerpts from "Jennie Lubell Is in a Nursing Home in Provincetown," *Sojourner*, August 1984.

Shirley Abbott, excerpts from *Womenfolks: Growing Up Down South*, Houghton Mifflin, 1983.

Pearl Buck, excerpts from *The Exile*, John Day, 1936.

Lorine Niedecker, excerpt from "HJ," T&G, The Jargon Society, 1968.

Anzia Yezierska, excerpts from *Bread Givers*, George Braziller, 1925; The Women's Press, 1984.

Agnes Smedley, excerpts from *Daughter of Earth* (1928), The Feminist Press, 1973; Virago Press, 1977.

Zora Neale Hurston, excerpts from *Dust Tracks on a Road.*

Helen Gardner, in *Elizabeth Cady Stanton—Susan B. Anthony: Correspondence, Writings, Speeches*, Schocken, 1981.

OCTOBER
Mournings, Elegies, Tributes

Cynthia Ozick, dedication to *Levitation*, Knopf, 1982; Secker & Warburg, 1982; Penguin, 1983.

Katherine Mansfield, excerpt from *Journals of Katherine Mansfield*, ed. by J. Middleton Murry, Knopf, 1956; Constable, 1984.

Emily Dickinson, excerpt from *The Letters of Emily Dickinson*, ed. by Thomas H. Johnson, Harvard University Press, 1965.

Lucille Clifton, excerpt from "Magic Mamma," *Good Times*, Random House, 1969.

Sources

Marge Piercy, excerpt from "My Mother's Body," *My Mother's Body,* Knopf (forthcoming 1985).

Judith Hemschemeyer, "My Mother's Death," *Very Close and Very Slow,* Wesleyan University Press, 1974.

Maude Meehan, excerpts from "Small Wings."

Hilary Sametz Lloyd, "Unveiling."

Nelly Sachs, "O My Mother," *The Seeker and Other Poems,* trans. by Ruth and Matthew Mead, Farrar, Straus and Giroux, 1970.

Katherine Doak, "Before I Slept," *New Poets: Women,* ed. by Terry Wetherby, Les Femmes/Celestial Arts, 1976.

Emily Dickinson, excerpts from *The Letters of Emily Dickinson.*

Emily Dickinson, "The Work of Her that went," *The Complete Poems of Emily Dickinson,* ed. by Thomas H. Johnson, Little, Brown, 1960; Faber, 1970.

Katherine Mansfield, excerpts from *Journals of Katherine Mansfield.*

Nellie Wong, excerpts from "Harbinger," *The Cow's Ear,* Blue Collar Press, 1977.

May Sarton, excerpts from "Of Grief," *Collected Poems of May Sarton, 1930–1973,* Norton, 1974.

Toby Talbot, excerpt from *A Book about My Mother,* Farrar, Straus and Giroux, 1980.

NOVEMBER
Legacies (As Is this All)

Judith Wright, excerpt from "Woman to Child," *The Double Tree: Selected Poems, 1942–1976,* Houghton Mifflin, 1978.

Anne Bradstreet, dedication, *The Works of Anne Bradstreet,* ed. by Jennine Hensley, Harvard University Press, 1967.

Joyce Carol Thomas, excerpts from "Bittersweet," *Bittersweet,* Firesign Press, 1973.

Sherley Anne Williams, "I Sing This Song for Our Mothers: Ruise," *The Peacock Poems,* Wesleyan University Press, 1975.

Zora Neale Hurston, excerpts from *Jonah's Gourd Vine,* from *I Love Myself When I Am Laughing . . . And Then Again When I Am Looking Mean and Impressive,* ed. by Alice Walker, The Feminist Press, 1979.

Betsy Sholl, excerpts from "Notes From a Youngest Daughter," *Changing Faces,* Alicejamesbooks, 1974.

Adele Wiseman, excerpts from *Old Woman at Play,* Clarke, Irwin, 1978.

Eudora Welty, excerpts from *One Writer's Beginnings,* Harvard University Press, 1984.

Sources

Sharon Doubiago, excerpts from "Mother," *Hard Country*, West End Press, 1982.

Dedications to: *This Bridge Called My Back: Writings by Radical Women of Color*, ed. by Cherrie Moraga and Gloria Anzaldua, Persephone, 1981; *Sturdy Black Bridges: Visions of Black Women in Literature* by Roseann P. Bell, Bettye J. Parker and Beverly Guy-Sheftall, Doubleday, 1979; *The Salt Eaters* by Toni Cade Bambara, Random, 1980; The Women's Press, 1982.

Toni Cade Bambara, excerpt from *Black Women Writers at Work,* ed. by Claudia Tate, Continuum Press, 1983.

Jessamyn West, excerpts from *Hide and Seek: A Continuing Journey*, Harcourt Brace Jovanovich, 1973.

Jessamyn West, excerpts from *The Woman Said Yes: Encounters with Life and Death*, Harcourt Brace Jovanovich, 1976.

Alice Walker, excerpts from *In Search of Our Mothers' Gardens: Womanist Prose*, Harcourt Brace Jovanovich, 1983.

Virginia Woolf, excerpts from *Moments of Being*, Harcourt Brace Jovanovich, 1976; Hogarth Press, 1976; Panther, 1978.

Colette, excerpts from *Earthly Paradise*, Farrar, Straus and Giroux, 1966; Secker & Warburg, 1966; Penguin, 1974.

DECEMBER
The Larger Caring: Dream Visions

Olive Schreiner, dedication to *Dreams*, Roberts Brothers, 1891; Wildwood House, 1982.

Tillie Olsen, excerpts from "Oh, Yes," *Tell Me a Riddle*, Delacorte, 1961; Virago Press, 1980.

Colette, excerpt from *Earthly Paradise*, Farrar, Straus and Giroux, 1966; Secker & Warburg, 1966; Penguin, 1974.

Adrienne Rich, excerpt from "Hunger," *The Dream of a Common Language, Poems 1974–1977*, Norton, 1978.

Alta, "I would be a fool to want more children," *Shameless Hussy: Selected Prose and Poetry*, The Crossing Press, 1980.

Tillie Olsen, "A Dream-Vision."

Susan Griffin, "The Awful Mother," *Made from This Earth: An Anthology of Writings*, Harper & Row, 1982; The Women's Press, 1982.

Julia Ward Howe, excerpts from "Appeal to Womanhood Throughout the World," *Julia Ward Howe* by Laura F. Richards and Maude Howe Elliot, Houghton Mifflin, 1915.

Sources

Julie Olsen Edwards, excerpts from "Motheroath," *Women's Studies Quarterly*, Summer 1984.

June Jordan, "Poem for South African Women," *Passion: New Poems, 1977–1980,* Beacon Press, 1980. (This poem was written in commemoration of the 40,000 women and children, who, August 9, 1956, presented themselves in bodily protest agains the "dompass" in the capital of apartheid. Presented at the United Nations, August 9, 1978.)

Nelly Sachs, "We Mothers," *The Seeker and Other Poems,* trans. by Ruth and Matthew Mead, Farrar, Straus and Giroux, 1970.

ACKNOWLEDGMENTS

We gratefully acknowledge permission to reprint the following material:

Shirley Abbott. Excerpts from *Womenfolks: Growing Up Down South* by Shirley Abbott reprinted by permission of Ticknor & Fields. Copyright © 1983 by Shirley Abbott, and the Wallace & Sheil Agency.

Ai. "But What I'm Trying to Say Mother Is" by Ai reprinted from her volume *Cruelty* by permission of Houghton Mifflin Company. Copyright © 1970, 1973 by Ai.

Paula Gunn Allen. "Grandmother" by Paula Gunn Allen reprinted by permission of the author from *The Third Woman: Minority Women Writers of the United States,* edited by Dexter Fisher, published by Houghton Mifflin. Copyright © 1977 by Paula Gunn Allen.

Alta. "49 Essays" and "I would be a fool to want more children" by Alta reprinted from her volume *Shameless Hussy: Selected Prose and Poetry* by permission of The Crossing Press.

Bryna Bar Oni. Excerpts from *The Vapor* by Bryna Bar Oni reprinted by permission of the author. Copyright © by Bryna Bar Oni.

Ellen Bass. "There Are Times in Life When One Does the Right Thing" and excerpts from "Our Stunning Harvest" printed by permission of the author. Copyright © by Ellen Bass.

Beth Brant. Excerpts from "A Long Story" by Beth Brant reprinted by permission of the author from *A Gathering of Spirit: Writing and Art by North American Indian Women,* edited by Beth Brant, published by Sinister Wisdom, Box 1023, Rockland, Maine, 04841.

Gwendolyn Brooks. Excerpts from "the mother" reprinted from *The World of Gwendolyn Brooks* by permission of Harper & Row, Publishers, Inc. Copyright © 1944, 1945 by Gwendolyn Brooks Blakely.

Lucille Clifton. Excerpt from "Magic Momma" by Lucille Clifton reprinted from her volume *Good Times* by permission of Random House, Inc. "February 13, 1980" by Lucille Clifton reprinted from her volume *Two-Headed Woman* by permission of Curtis Brown, Ltd. Copyright © 1980 by the University of Massachusetts Press.

Jane Cooper. "My Young Mother" by Jane Cooper reprinted with permission

Acknowledgments

of Macmillan Publishing Company and Anvil Press Poetry Ltd., from *Scaffolding: New and Selected Poems of Jane Cooper*. Copyright © 1968, 1969 by Jane Cooper. Originally appeared in *Voyages*.

Patricia Cumming. "Caesura" and "Spring" by Patricia Cumming reprinted by permission of the author from her volume *Letter from an Outlying Province*, published by Alicejamesbooks.

Laura Davis. Excerpts from "Things You Gave Me" printed by permission of Laura Davis. Copyright © by Laura Davis.

Emily Dickinson. Excerpts reprinted by permission of the publishers from *The Letters of Emily Dickinson*, edited by Thomas H. Johnson, Cambridge, Mass.: The Belknap Press of Harvard University Press, Copyright © 1951, 1958 by the President and Fellows of Harvard College. "The Work of Her that went" reprinted by permission of the publishers and the Trustees of Amherst College from *The Poems of Emily Dickinson*, edited by Thomas H. Johnson, Cambridge, Mass.: The Belknap Press of Harvard University Press, Copyright © 1951, 1955, 1979, 1983 by the President and Fellows of Harvard College.

Katherine Doak. "Before I Slept" by Katherine Doak reprinted from *New Poets: Women*, edited by Terry Wetherby, by permission of Celestial Arts/Les Femmes.

Sharon Doubiago. Excerpts from "Mother" by Sharon Doubiago reprinted from her volume *Hard Country* by permission of West End Press.

Carolyn Forche. Excerpts from "Burning the Tomato Worms" by Carolyn Forche reprinted from her volume *Gathering of the Tribe* by permission of the author and Yale University Press. © 1976 by Carolyn Forche.

Celia Gilbert. "Circles" by Celia Gilbert reprinted from *The Women's Review of Books* 1:8 (May 1984) by permission of the author and *The Women's Review of Books*. Copyright © Celia Gilbert.

Susan Griffin. "Rebecca" by Susan Griffin printed by permission of the author. Copyright © by Susan Griffin. "The Awful Mother" by Susan Griffin reprinted from her volume *Made from This Earth: An Anthology of Writings* by permission of the author and The Women's Press. Copyright © 1982 by Susan Griffin.

Kay Keeshan Hamod. Excerpts from "Transitions" by Kay Keeshan Hamod reprinted by permission of the author from *Working It Out: 23 Women Artists, Scientists, and Scholars Talk about Their Lives and Work*, edited by Sara Ruddick and Pamela Daniels, published by Random House.

Jana Harris. "When Mama Came Here as a Gold Panner" by Jana Harris reprinted from her volume *Manhattan as a Second Language and Other Poems* by permission of Harper & Row, Publishers, Inc. Copyright © 1982 by Jana Harris.

Acknowledgments

Judith Hemschemeyer. "My Mother's Death" by Judith Hemschemeyer reprinted from her volume *Very Close and Very Slow* by permission of Wesleyan University Press. Copyright © 1975 by Judith Hemschemeyer Rosenfeld.

Laurel O. Hoye. "You Are . . ." printed by permission of the author. Copyright © by Laurel O. Hoye.

June Jordan. "Poem for South African Women" by June Jordan reprinted from her volume *Passion: New Poems, 1977–1980* by permission of Beacon Press. Copyright © 1980 by June Jordan.

Shirley Kaufman. Excerpts from "Apples" by Shirley Kaufman reprinted from her volume *Gold Country* by permission of the University of Pittsburgh Press. Copyright © 1973 by Shirley Kaufman. "I Hear You" by Shirley Kaufman reprinted from her volume *The Floor Keeps Turning* by permission of the University of Pittsburgh Press. Copyright © 1970 by the University of Pittsburgh Press.

Carolyn Kizer. Excerpts from "The Blessing" by Carolyn Kizer reprinted by permission of the author from her volume *Yin: New Poems*, published by BOA Editions.

Maxine Kumin. "The Jouney: For Jane at Thirteen" by Maxine Kumin reprinted from her volume *Our Ground Time Here Will Be Brief* by permission of Viking Penguin, Inc. and Curtis Brown, Ltd.

Audre Lorde. "Story Books on a Kitchen Table" by Audre Lord reprinted from her volume *Coal* by permission of W. W. Norton, Inc. Copyright © 1968, 1970, 1976 by Audre Lorde. "Black Mother Woman" and excerpts from "Teacher" by Audre Lorde reprinted by permission of the author from her volume *From a Land Where Other People Live*, published by Broadside Press.

Hilary Sametz Lloyd. "Unveiling" by Hilary Sametz Lloyd printed by permission of the author. Copyright © by Hilary Sametz Lloyd.

Katie McBain. Excerpts from "I Want To Be Your Daughter Now" by Katie McBain printed by permission of the author. Copyright © by Katie McBain.

Laureen Mar. "My Mother, Who Came from China, Where She Never Saw Snow" and "Chinatown 4" reprinted from *The Third Woman: Minority Women Writers of the United States*, edited by Dexter Fisher, published by Houghton Mifflin. Copyright © 1977 by Laureen Mar.

Stephanie Markman. Excerpts from "and/mother why did you tell me" by Stephanie Markman reprinted by permission of the author from *One Foot on the Mountain*, edited by Lillian Mohin, published by Onlywomen Press. Copyright © by Stephanie Markman.

Margaret Mead. Excerpts from "That I not be a restless ghost" by Margaret

288

Acknowledgments

Mead reprinted from her volume *Blackberry Winter* by permission of William Morrow & Company, and Angus & Robertson Ltd. Copyright © 1972 by Margaret Mead.

Maude Meehan. Excerpts from "Small Wings" by Maude Meehan reprinted by permission of the author from *Moonjuice IV*, edited by Sharon Gladden, published by Embers Press.

Janice Mirikitani. Excerpts from "Sing with Your Body" by Janice Mirikitani reprinted by permission of the author from her volume *Awake in the River*, published by Isthmus Press. Copyright © 1978 by Janice Mirikitani.

Cherrie Moraga. Excerpts from "La Dolce Culpa" by Cherrie Moraga reprinted by permission of the author from her volume *Loving in the War Years: Lo Que Nunca Paso por sus Labios*, published by South End Press, 302 Columbus Avenue, Boston, MA 02116. Copyright © by Cherrie Moraga.

Alice Munro. Excerpts from "Winter Wind" by Alice Munro reprinted from her volume *Something I've Been Meaning to Tell You* by permission of Virginia Barber Literary Agency, Inc.

Michele Murray. Excerpts from "Dance Poem" and "Poem of Two" by Michele Murray reprinted from her volume *The Great Mother and Other Poems* by permission of James Murray.

Adeline Naiman. Excerpts from "Jennie Lubell Is in a Nursing Home in Provincetown" by Adeline Naiman reprinted from *Sojourner* (August 1984) by permission of the author. Copyright © by Adeline Naiman.

Lorine Niedecker. Excerpts from poem "HJ" by Lorine Niedecker reprinted from her volume *T & G* by permission of The Jargon Society.

Sharon Olds. "35/10" by Sharon Olds reprinted from her volume *The Dead and the Living* by permission of the author and Alfred A. Knopf, Inc. Copyright © 1982 by Sharon Olds.

Tillie Olsen. "A Dream-Vision" by Tillie Olsen printed by permission of the author. Copyright © by Tillie Olsen.

Lady Otomo of Sakanoue. "Sent from the Capital to Her Elder Daughter" by Lady Otomo of Sakanoue reprinted by permission of Penguin Books Ltd. from *The Penguin Book of Japanese Verse*, trans. by Anthony Thwaite and Geoffrey Bownas. Copyright © Geoffrey Bownas and Anthony Thwaite.

Grace Paley. Excerpts from "Mom" by Grace Paley reprinted by permission of the author. Copyright © by Grace Paley. Previously published in *Esquire* and *Feminist Studies*.

Theresa Palma Acosta. Excerpts from "My Mother Pieced Quilts" by Theresa Palma Acosta reprinted from her volume *Festival de Flor y Canto* by permission of the University of Southern California.

Marge Piercy. Excerpts from "My Mother's Body" by Marge Piercy printed by

289

Acknowledgments

permission of the author. Copyright © by Marge Piercy. Excerpts from "My Mother's Novel" by Marge Piercy reprinted from her volume *The Moon Is Always Female* reprinted by permission of Alfred A. Knopf, Inc. Copyright © 1980 by Marge Piercy.

Sylvia Plath. "Child" by Sylvia Plath reprinted from *Winter Trees* by permission of Faber & Faber Ltd. Copyright © 1971 by Ted Hughes.

Marie Ponsot. Excerpts from "Nursing: Mother" by Marie Ponsot reprinted from her volume *Admit Impediment* by permission of Alfred A. Knopf, Inc. Copyright © 1977 by Marie Ponsot.

Adrienne Rich. Exerpt "Mary Gravely Jones" from "Grandmothers" by Adrienne Rich reprinted from her volume *A Wild Patience Has Taken Me This Far, Poems 1978–1981* by permission of W. W. Norton & Company, Inc. Copyright © 1981 by Adrienne Rich. Exerpt from "Hunger" by Adrienne Rich reprinted from her volume *The Dream of a Common Language, Poems 1974–1977* by permission of W. W. Norton & Company, Inc. Copyright © 1978 by W. W. Norton & Company, Inc.

Del Marie Rogers. "Desert" by Del Marie Rogers reprinted by permission of the author from *New Poets: Women*, edited by Terry Wetherby, published by Les Femmes/Celestial Arts. First published in *The New Salt Creek Reader*, edited by Ted Kooser. Copyright © by Del Marie Rogers.

Muriel Rukeyser. "Night Feeding" reprinted from *Selected Poems of Muriel Rukeyser* by permission of International Creative Management, Inc. Copyright © 1951, 1979 by Muriel Rukeyser.

Nelly Sachs. "O My Mother," and "We Mothers" by Nelly Sachs by permission of Suhrkamp Verlag.

May Sarton. Excerpts from "Of Grief" by May Sarton reprinted from *The Collected Poems of May Sarton, 1930–1973* by permission of W. W. Norton & Company, Inc. and Russell & Volkening, Inc. Copyright © 1974 by May Sarton.

Hannah Senesh. "To My Mother" by Hannah Senesh reprinted from *Hannah Senesh: Her Life and Diary* by permission of Schocken Books, Inc. and Valentine Mitchell & Co. Copyright © 1966 by Hakibbutz Publishing House Ltd. English edition copyright © 1971 by Nigel Marsh.

Betsy Sholl. Excerpts from "Notes from a Youngest Daughter" by Betsy Sholl reprinted by permission of the author from her volume *Changing Faces*, published by Alicejamesbooks.

Judith Sornberger. "Thinking of My Mother Who Fifteen Years Later, Has Gone East to See the Leaves" and "The Place to Begin" by Judith Sornberger printed by permission of the author. Copyright © by Judith Sornberger.

Rosalie Sorrels. Excerpts from "Apple of My Eye" by Rosalie Sorrels reprinted

Acknowledgments

by permission of Music Management from *What, Woman, and Who, Myself, I Am*, edited by Rosalie Sorrels, published by Wooden Shoe.

Sue Standing. Excerpts from "Cellar Door" by Sue Standing reprinted by permission of the author from her volume *Amphibious Weather*, published by Zephyr Press.

Gloria Steinem. Excerpts from "Ruth's Song (Because She Could Not Sing It)" by Gloria Steinem reprinted by permission of the author from her volume *Outrageous Acts and Everyday Rebellions*, published by Holt, Rinehart and Winston, Jonathan Cape.

May Stevens. Excerpts from *Ordinary/Extraordinary* by May Stevens reprinted by permission of the author. Copyright © by May Stevens.

Ruth Stone. "Advice" by Ruth Stone reprinted from her volume *Topography and Other Poems* by permission of Harcourt Brace Jovanovich, Inc. Copyright © 1971 by Ruth Stone.

Joyce Carol Thomas. Excerpts from "Bittersweet" by Joyce Carol Thomas reprinted by permission of the author from her volume *Bittersweet*, published by Firesign Press.

Alice Walker. "Foregiveness" by Alice Walker reprinted from her volume *Good Night Willie Lee I'll See You in the Morning* by permission of Julian Bach Literary Agency, Inc. Copyright © 1975 by Alice Walker.

Jeanne Murray Walker. Excerpt from "For My Daughter's Twenty-First Birthday" by Jeanne Murray Walker reprinted by permission of the author and the University of Iowa Press from *Extended Outlooks: The Iowa Review Collection of Contemporary Women Writers*, edited by Jane Cooper, published by Macmillan Publishing Company. Copyright © by Iowa Review.

Jessamyn West. Excerpts from *Hide and Seek: A Continuing Journey* by Jessamyn West reprinted by permission of Harcourt Brace Jovanovich, Inc. Copyright © 1973 by Jessamyn West.

Sherley Anne Williams. "The Peacock Poems: 1" and "I Sing This Song for Our Mothers: Ruise" by Sherley Anne Williams reprinted from her volume *The Peacock Poems* by permission of Wesleyan University Press. Copyright © 1975 by Sherley Williams.

Adele Wiseman. Excerpts from *Old Woman at Play* by Adele Wiseman reprinted by permission of the author. Copyright © by Adele Wiseman.

Nellie Wong. Excerpt from "From a Heart of Rice Straw" by Nellie Wong reprinted by permission of the author from her volume *Dreams in Harrison Railroad Park*, published by Kelsey Street Press. Excerpts from "Harbinger" by Nellie Wong reprinted by permission of the author from her volume *The Cow's Ear*, published by Blue Collar Press. Excerpts from "Red Journeys" by Nellie Wong printed by permission of the author. Copyright © by Nellie Wong.

Acknowledgments

Virginia Woolf. Excerpts from *Moments of Being* by Virginia Woolf reprinted by permission of the author's estate and The Hogarth Press. Copyright © by Quentin Bell and Angelica Garnett.

Judith Wright. "Woman to Child" by Judith Wright reprinted from her volume *The Double Tree* by permission of Houghton Mifflin Company and Angus & Robertson Publishers. Copyright © 1978 by Judith Wright.

INDEX TO WRITERS

Index to Writers